Paola Ravasio

# This Train is Not Bound for Glory

## A Study of Literary Trainscapes

T0308611

INTER-AMERICAN STUDIES
Cultures – Societies – History

ESTUDIOS INTERAMERICANOS
Culturas – Sociedades – Historia

Volume 36

Paola Ravasio

# This Train is Not Bound for Glory

## A Study of Literary Trainscapes

uuut Wissenschaftlicher Verlag Trier

Copublished by
**UNO** University of New Orleans Press

This Train is Not Bound for Glory.
A Study of Literary Trainscapes /
Paola Ravasio. –
(Inter-American Studies | Estudios Interamericanos; 36)
Trier: WVT Wissenschaftlicher Verlag Trier, 2021
ISBN 978-3-86821-836-7
New Orleans, LA: University of New Orleans Press, 2021
ISBN 978-1-60801-216-9

SPONSORED BY THE

Federal Ministry
of Education
and Research

The project, on which this book is based, has been funded by the German Federal Ministry of Education and Research (Bundesministerium für Bildung und Forschung, BMBF). The responsibility for the content of this publication lies with the author.

Cover Image: Railway tracks in Calle Blancos, San José, Costa Rica, Paola Ravasio (2017)
Cover Design: Brigitta Disseldorf

Library of Congress Cataloging-in-Publication Data
Names: Ravasio, Paola, author.
Title: This train is not bound for glory : a study of literary trainscapes /
Paola Ravasio.
Description: Trier : Wissenschaftlicher Verlag ; New Orleans, LA :
University of New Orleans Press, 2021. | Series: Inter-American studies;
36 | Includes bibliographical references.
Identifiers: LCCN 2020044526 | ISBN 9781608012169 (paperback)
Subjects: LCSH: Central American literature--History and criticism. |
Central America--Emigration and immigration--Social aspects. |
Emigration and immigration in literature. | Social mobility in
literature. | Railroad travel in literature. | Railroads in literature.
Classification: LCC PQ7471 .R38 2021 | DDC 860.9/9728--dc23
LC record available at https://lccn.loc.gov/2020044526

© WVT Wissenschaftlicher Verlag Trier, 2021

Publisher: WVT Wissenschaftlicher Verlag Trier, Postfach 4005, D-54230 Trier,
Bergstraße 27, D-54295 Trier, Tel. 0049 651 41503, Fax 41504, www.wvttrier.de, wvt@wvttrier.de

Copublisher: University of New Orleans Press, 2000 Lakeshore Drive, Earl K. Long Library,
Room 221, New Orleans, LA 70148, United States, 504-280-7457, unopress.org

# Table of Contents

# Introduction

*...las Américas – Tierras de Lágrimas*
Cubena, *Chombo*

The literary representation of the railway system is highly useful for visualizing mobility and the social world as correlated entities in the Americas. Understood here as the conjunction of the social and the mobile, *literary trainscapes* underscore modern displacement as being at the heart of a complex matrix of traits, patterns, and structures of societal (trans)formations. Deployed by the novels' own narrative textuality, trainscapes are constituted as an intertwining of pictorial representations constructed around the train. They are complex narrative nodes represented around the mobility of human and material capital by the railway system, which are both interdependent on the economies moving that capital. The following pages aim to demonstrate how trainscapes (also, *tsc*) correlate train-caused spatial and social im/mobilities by considering how the dynamic relations between bodies, movement, and money are depicted in the chosen narratives to be explored next.

The meaningful content literary *tsc* withhold regarding the correlation of the social and the mobile in different historical imaginations of the Central American region is composed across two overlapping arrangements. *Infrastructurally*, they depict scenarios, people, goods, and histories in movement conjoining the *train-people-money* triad across movement and standstill. *Informationally*, tsc deploy a circulation rhetoric (cf. Tsing 2002) where mobility encapsulates social content and dynamics across movement, economic exploitation, and political (ir)regulation. Under this framework of thought, *tsc* mirror Mimi Sheller's claim that "mobility systems are informational as much as they are infrastructural" (2014, 799) and are hence approached here as metaphors (from Greek μεταφορά) exemplifying systems of mobilities, immobilities and moorings (cf. Hannam, Sheller, and Urry 2006). Understood as the transferal of a word to a new meaning, metaphors *bear* or *carry* (Gr. φέρω) a connotation that has been transferred from one significant to (Gr. μετά) the other.[1] In this sense, *tsc* are metaphorical insofar they *carry* the conjunction of the social and the mobile in the form of the *train-world*, which across these pages indicates the triad *train-people-money*. Here, the social is represented as a 'hybrid geography of materialities' composed by the interaction between machine-bodies-money, which coexists and is codependent with differentiated practices of mobility (Hannam, Sheller, and Urry 2006, 14). As a consequence, literary *tsc* depict "social kinetics" (cf. Bryson 2003, 75) that reveal how mobility operates within fields of power, sketching how movement of human and material capital are represented both as products, as producers of power (Cresswell 2006). Trainscapes, therefore, are not reduced solely to the portrayal of the train, itself rather unlimited in its semiotic potential.

Representing modernity's first mechanized mass transit scheme (Harrington 2000), the railway system revolutionized (that is, 'annihilated') the concepts of space and time in the nineteenth century (Schivelbusch 2014). Even though human mobility was just as central to ancient empires as it was to power structures of early modernity (Sheller 2014), the movement of people, information, and material goods underwent revolutionary transformations with the *iron horse*. In fact, "the train acted as a metonym for modernity – its very existence testified to the presence and legitimacy of the modern" (Aguiar 2008, 71), thus inaugurating modernity as "an obsessive march forwards" (Bauman 1990, 10). Like other systems of mobility, the railroad transported things and people from one place to another. What distinguished it radically from these, however, was the fact that *route* and *vehicle* became one and the same with the railway (Schivelbusch 2014, 16). While on the other hand, the lim-

---

1    In the *Poetics* (1457b), Aristotle defines metaphor as "the application of a strange term either transferred from the genus and applied to the species or from the species and applied to the genus, or from one species to another or else by analogy. [...] Metaphor by analogy means this: when B is to A as D is to C, then instead of B the poet will say D and B instead of D."

ited materiality of past mobilities was replaced with the qualities of *speed*, *intensity*, and *technological* means (cf. Sheller 2014, 794 and Aguiar 2008). Aspects that necessarily led to the significant compression of the space-time vectors, bringing people and places closer together. This would modify societies drastically from the point of view of connectivity, as well as enhance the development of industrial capitalism in the decades to come. As a counterpart of nineteenth century processes of industrialization and modernization, such innovations paved the way for the railway system to transform societies and their economies precisely from the new mobilities it implemented. As elaborated upon by Harrington (2000), the railway system not only signified the industrialization of speed and travel by way of a great mobile machine hauling carriages while gliding upon wheels and rails. People as passengers – and by extension experiences of sociality and social structures alike – underwent fundamental transformations.

Inherently connected to an ideology of progress, the new possibilities of mobility conveyed by the train embodied ideals of freedom, of socioeconomic betterment, and of having a democratizing, levelling effect on society (Harrington 2000, 229-231). Harrington also expands on Schivelbusch's excursus on railway-caused pathologies such as industrial fatigue and shock, and elaborates upon the new neurotic subjectivities of modernity as consequence of the train journey.[2] Above all, he underscores how travelling by train in nineteenth-century Victorian society became a collective experience that reshaped social relations and spaces altogether, mainly by converting private and individual experience into one of mass public sociality, notes Schivelbusch (cf. Bissell 2009). Broader and ampler social interaction was possible due to new spaces like railroad stations, the platform, train carriages, and the communal journey itself, all of

---

2    The author mentions fear of social mixing, the potential for disorder and violence, as well as assault and crime, regulation and control, and the stress of punctuality as examples thereof. These aspects influenced people's health in new ways, producing new affected subjectivities (i.e. anxiety, pressure, stress, exhaustion, and fear).

which revolutionized the concept and physical practice of displacement across new dynamics of "being-with-others" (Bissell 2009).
Bearing the strain of plural societies on the move, the railway system amplified the dimensions of social interaction across circulation, exchange, and travel. Social experience was hence transformed
by way of mobility and displacement. It became fluid and mechanized, and inevitably developed different social spaces within new,
modern societies. As the railway system expanded across the globe
in the nineteenth century under the mantle of European colonial
empire-building and U.S. colonization processes (Thompson 2014,
214), Latin American countries also attempted to enter the grand
narrative of progress by way of the modernized transportation system. In these processes, mobilities and social realities transformed
themselves contiguously as people, machines, money, ideas, and
power became mobile in an exponential fashion (Sheller and Urry
2006). Socioeconomic networks were thus transformed by techno-
logically enhanced mobility.

The present discussion follows an inter-American study of literary trainscapes in order to approach interconnected and transversal sociohistorical entanglements in the Americas (cf. Raussert
2014). *This Train is Not Bound for Glory* aligns itself with the
emergent field of inter-American studies given that, as explained by
Olaf Kaltmeier in *The Routledge Handbook to the History and Society of the Americas* (2019), the field "perceive[s] the Americas as
multiply entangled, interconnected, and shaped by historical power
relations" (5). Something that literary trainscapes reveal across their
intertextual composition. The field has also challenged the ways of
thinking about the region beyond fixed notions like 'North' and
'South', creating instead a "model of horizontal dialogue" between
Latin American, Caribbean, and North American (U.S. and Canada)
Studies (Raussert 2015, 2). As underscored by Wilfried Raussert in
the introduction of *The Routledge Companion to Inter-American
Studies* (2017), the field focuses on the regions' juxtapositions,
overlapping, and layers of historical concurrences that the prefix *in-
ter-* implies (cf. Luz 2006, 146). As a result, the field conceptualizes

the Americas "as historically, culturally, politically, and economically *entangled*" (Raussert 2017, 3; emphasis added). *The Routledge Handbook* Series, edited by the Center for InterAmerican Studies (CIAS) at the University of Bielefeld on subjects such as history and society in the Americas (Kaltmeier et al. 2019), culture and media of the Americas (Raussert et al. 2019), and political economy and governance in the region (Kaltmeier et al. 2020) emphasize and develop the need for such refreshing inter-American perspectives.

Accordingly, the ensuing pages inspect entwined spaces and histories of the Americas by engaging the literary representation of the train-world from such premises. In so doing, the present study approaches the Americas as a space of entanglements and aims to make visible the multidimensional overlapping and multidirectional interactions that have interwoven the region across time and space. Which is why *This Train is Not Bound for Glory* also takes part in the development of the field itself. It explores in fact the '*mobile and entangled America(s)*' (cf. Graham and Raussert 2016) by way of the railway system and from a hemispheric lens. A lens that aims furthermore to reveal those historical relations of power that have consolidated the entangled Americas due to mobile transnational economies along categories of repetition, fragmentation, and inequality. The main contention here is that literary trainscapes highlight structures of power asymmetry, interconnectedness, and transversal relations in the Americas (cf. Raussert 2017, 11), representing moreover an interesting trope for the inter-American paradigm overall. Lastly, given that "[m]igration and flows have increasingly shaped most recent social, economic, and cultural developments in the Americas" (Raussert 2015, 8), *mobility*, one of the key tropes in inter-American studies, is central to the present study.

Determined to a great degree by the *mobility turn* that has taken place in the social sciences in the last decades, issues of intersecting movements and mobilities have become the focus of contemporary discussions regarding the multifold structures of modernity – *the social* being of innovative importance. The editors of *The Routledge*

*Handbook of Mobilities* (2014) explain how a 'material turn' in the social sciences and humanities has inevitably led scholars to rethink what the social might actually be, reconfiguring it as 'mobile' (Adey et al. 2014, 12). Understood by Tim Cresswell (2010) as structural dynamics "between classes, genders, ethnicities, [and] nationalities" (21), the social is now being approached in the social sciences and the humanities from the perspective that underscores the predominant role mobility has in installing an intricate relationality of places, goods, and people. This complex interaction is furthermore co-produced, practiced, and represented in relation to mobilities and moorings that are gender-, race-, and class-determined (Sheller 2014, 795). Mobility, therefore, is seen as being in essence a social phenomenon (Urry 2000) constructed in interdependence with spatial and social mobility,[3] which necessarily entails a reciprocal relationship with the political, economic, and ethical dimensions of uneven movement (Sheller 2014). Opposed to traditional static theory and research in the social sciences, the new mobilities paradigm attempts to shed light upon differentiated mobility and its effect in the social world, and vice versa (Sheller 2014; Sheller and Urry 2006).

By proposing literary trainscapes as an interdisciplinary category of analysis for scrutinizing the Americas as a space of entanglements on the one hand, the ensuing discussion rethinks the social in the Americas by way of the train-world on the other. *This Train is Not Bound for Glory* focuses hence on the portrayal of the narratives' social dynamics drawing on the representation of uneven practices of train-related mobility, which are defined moreover by the flows of U.S. transnational capitalism in Central America. Lastly, *tsc* are examined here with the purpose of revealing how the literary representation of the train-world correlates *spatial* displacement and standstill with *social* immobility, thus expanding on the discussion of the social in the Americas – "considered one of the most socially

---

3    For a discussion on the differences and intersections between social and spatial mobility, see Kaufmann, Bergman, and Joye 2004, 746-749. See also Hannam, Sheller, and Urry 2006.

Introduction 7

unjust regions in the world" (Kaltmeier and Breuer 2020, 205). As a result, the ensuing analysis extracts a *dialectics of im/mobilities* from the chosen storylines by asking, fundamentally, in what ways do literary trainscapes elucidate the way power is constructed and entangled in the Americas across mobility? Who intersect at literary trainscapes, where, and how? What are the mobile metaphors for (neo)colonialism, (anti)imperialism, and oppression? What kind of economies perpetuate these? Which movements counteract and oppose them?

Displacement and mobilities are indeed a central aspect of historical and contemporary existence (Sheller 2014). It is hence not by chance that Cresswell has indicated that the "foundational narratives of modernity have been constructed around the brute fact of moving" (2010, 21). That which differs between these narratives, clarifies the author, are however the meanings and representations ascribed to the practices of movement, which are historically and geographically specific. Mobilities and moorings figure differently depending on the national spaces and historical periods they belong to (Skeggs 2004, 48), becoming thus culturally and socially encoded in their representations (Cresswell 2010, 20). History and ideology implicate together such codes. Cresswell's illustration of the minstrel, the vagabond, and the pilgrim in feudal Europe exemplifies how their social meanings and representations as a "class of mobile masterless men" were constructed as socially and morally threatening opposite the established order. Contrarily, the discourses constructed around modern mobilities defined by new means of transportation like the railway system, were conjoined to morally positive connotations of freedom, liberty, and progress (27).

As metaphors representing systems of mobility and moorings, *tsc* endure too modifications in their representations and meanings according to the systematic and historically contingent crystallizations of their content and form, making them plural. Their varied literary representations make evident how their narrative encoding corresponds to specific historical imaginations. Which is why trainscapes are examined here as metaphors of im/mobility that withhold a substructure of historical meaning from which social content can be extracted in order to study the mobile entanglements of the Americas.[4] It must be however underscored that, despite such divergencies, literary trainscapes sketch altogether train-derived social kinetics that portray nonetheless striking parallels across their differences. These point to the juxtapositions and overlapping occurrences entangling the Americas, comprising both the sociohistorical processes of the past (*res gestae*) as the region's literary production referring to that past (*res gestarum*), what is meant here by 'historical imagination'.

Drawing from the fact that mobilities orchestrate new interactions between actors and structures in specific contexts, the present study engages the literary representation of the train-world in three different Central American historical imaginations in conjunction with the U.S. These refer to the construction of the Panama Canal, to the presence of the United Fruit Company in Central America, and lastly to the contemporary human caravan traversing Mexico towards the U.S. border. This inter-American approach explores *tsc* as an object of historical contemplation, one that projects in each reformulation the historicity of its content accordingly to the motives, needs, and interests of particular writers in specific moments and places. Because of this, the narratives' train-world is deciphered accordingly to the historical and geographical particularities of the

---

4    See Blumenberg (*Paradigms for a Metaphorology* 2010), who affirms "metaphors can also ... be *foundational elements* of philosophical language" (2010, 6). These, he goes on to state, undergo transformations according to the "metakinetics of the historical horizons of meaning" (Ibid.). Like concepts, hence, metaphors endure modifications in their representations and meanings because they originate in rather specific historical conditions, having thus "a *history*" of their own (34). Carrying out a *metaphorology* of intellectual emblems like that of the *cave* in Western thought, Blumenberg proposes a critical reflection that traces the metaphor's particular *substructure of underground meaning* by placing it in relation with its conceptual history (6). In this study, trainscapes are placed in relation with the sociohistorical processes that the narratives recreate so as to engage its substructure of historical meaning.

stories been told – both fictional as factual – taking into account a "specific historical-political plurilocal context" (Kaltmeier 2019, 2) and scrutinizing it through a hemispheric lens that helps grasp the transnational and inter-American dimensions comprising the Americas of a space of entanglements. A comparative hermeneutic of *tsc* therefore brings to the surface an intertextual dialectics of im/mobility from which a relational framework is construed between various sociohistorical scenarios, tracing above all how mobility does not exist as abstract movement nor decontextualized from power differentials (Cresswell 2006).

Since mobility is seen as being directly related to connectivity and empowerment, but also to disconnection and social exclusion (Sheller 2014), the purpose here is to demonstrate how mobility is central to the production and reproduction of power relations in the indicated narratives (Cresswell 2010). Following Doreen Massey (1993), "power geometries" correspond to the ways different social groups and individuals relate to mobility, underlining *power* as a central feature differentiating these relations. In the author's own words, "some [social groups or individuals] are more in charge of [mobility] than others; some initiate flows and movement, others don't; some are more on the receiving end of it than others; some are effectively imprisoned by it" (61). The ensuing analysis aims to disclose how *tsc* portray mobility installed, carried out, and located within fields of power coding in the form of "kinetic hierarchies" (Cresswell 2010, 26). These mirror how "mobility and control over mobility both reflect and reinforce power", as Skeggs underscores in his book *Class, Self, Culture* (2004, 49). As the author points out, not everyone has the same relationship to mobility while 'on the move'.

The capacity to be mobile in social and geographic spaces is directly related to differentiated access, skills and competences, and to the effective appropriation of the aforementioned qualities, which are all necessary for socio-spatial mobility. Kaufmann, Bergman, and Joye (2004) have termed this "motility". Assessed by Hannam, Sheller, and Urry as "a crucial dimension of unequal power rela-

tions" (2004, 3), motility has to do with the capacity that entities
have to become mobile, be them people, goods, or information.
This, however, is interdependent with the ways such entities are
able to access and embody socio-spatial mobility according to their
circumstances (Kaufmann, Bergman, and Joye 2004, 750). Hence,
the authors elucidate the concept under the rubric "mobility as capital", underlining the unequal distribution of access, skills, and possibilities such entities have regarding physical, social, and political
opportunities to become mobile (Sheller 2014, 797). Drawing on
social kinetics, kinetic hierarchies, and motility as intrinsic elements
of power geometries, the ensuing pages outline *tsc* as a dialectics of
im/mobility which create hierarchies of social classes and, in a reciprocal manner, social hierarchies of mobility.

The present study is structured in three parts that arrange an
intertextuality of male, female, and child mobilities along qualities
of speed, friction, and stagnation. Each chapter carries out a hermeneutic of the literary depictions of mobilities and standstill in the
fictional pieces, extracting mobile metaphors that project a circulation rhetoric. Part I, "Laying the Tracks", focuses on Carlos "Cubena" Guillermo Wilson's novel *Chombo* (1981). This section extracts a dialectics of im/mobility from three chosen storylines which
deploy a circulation rhetoric composed by departure from the homeland and frustrated dreams of homegoing in relation with obstructed
upward mobility for Blacks in Panama. Here, trainscapes deploy the
social world as caught between diaspora[5] and the Panamanian imag-

---

5    In *Global Diasporas* (2008), Cohen outlines "four phases of diaspora
     studies" and explains "Diaspora" in singular and in capital letters as re-
     ferring to a first phase, which originally was circumscribed to the Jewish
     experience. The author discusses how Safran (1991) reconfigured this
     exclusivity and expanded the concept to comprise a more wide-ranging
     group of people in displacement, such as expatriates and political refu-
     gees (second phase). According to Cohen, the 1990s witnessed a third
     reconstitution of the concept influenced by postmodern theory. The con-
     ceptual baggage of 'diasporas' was then transformed into a more "flexi-
     ble and situational" construction (2008, 5). Currently, Diaspora Studies
     incorporate deterritorialized postmodern conceptions, while still under-

ined community (Anderson 1996) due to racial considerations of citizenship that marginalized the migrant workforce who later became *Afro-Central American*.[6] The second part, "All Aboard?", draws on the "revenge of the still" (cf. Bissel and Fuller 2009) and focuses on immobility and social standstill as portrayed in three texts pertaining to the *banana novel* genre: "Bananos y hombres" (Lyra 2011 [1931]), *Bananos* (Quintana 2002 [1942]), and *Prisión Verde* (Amaya Amador 1957 [1950]). Opposite the ideal of free movement and circulation intrinsic to the symbology of the railway system, entrapment characterizes these novels along the lines of captivity, moribund displacement, and hindered social mobility for the *peones* of the United Fruit Company's mobile banana economy. Part three instead carries out a detailed hermeneutic of the representation of the freight train colloquially referred to as '*La Bestia*' in the opening poem of Rodrigo Balam's anthology entitled *Libro centroamericano de los muertos* (2018). "Riding the Beast" thus focuses on displacement and experiences of stillness of undocumented Central American migrants traversing Mexico by exploring the mobile metaphors of crucifixion, disappearance, and ouroboric, that is, cyclical mobilities (from Gr. ουροβόρος). The social shall be approached and defined in each section by the intersection of social

---

scoring the 'homeland' as central to the constitution of diasporas (cf. Ravasio 2020, 28).

6    When defining "Afro-Costa Rican", anthropologist Michael Olien distinguished between "African Blacks" (the slave labor force of colonial times), "West Indian Blacks" (Caribbean proletarian workers at the United Fruit Company, mainly Jamaicans), and "Costa Rican Blacks" (Costa Rican-born Blacks who have been recognized as Costa Rican citizens since 1949). I draw on Olien's classification and use "Afro-Central Americans" along the same lines in order to refer exclusively to the descendants of this insular Afro-Caribbean migrant workforce that resettled in Central America in the twentieth century (Michael Olien n.d., quoted in Herzfeld 1978 and 1994). For a discussion regarding the concept of "Afro-Central American-ness" and the role of dislocation and translocation between the isthmus and the Caribbean archipelago, see Muñoz Muñoz (2019).

and spatial im/mobilities determined by the train-world, whose circulation rhetoric is derived from the narrativization of departure, displacement, and arrival.

Lastly, it must not go without mentioning that the title of the present study finds its inspiration in the gospel song "This Train is Bound for Glory".[7] The content matter of the song praises a spiritual journey in which the train represents a metaphor of freedom and a symbol of liberation (Floyd 1993, 36), which is why *glory* represents the desired destination. That is, a state of existential bliss and prosperity. However, since the ensuing analysis of literary trainscapes underscores a reality which contradicts fully what the title asserts, the negating adverb "not" has been purposively incorporated in order to accentuate the nature of the social world here analyzed. Sure enough, the study's main contention sustains trainscapes depict a narrative of the mobile outcasts of modernity, thus portraying why 'this train is *not* bound for glory'. Rather, recalling the epigraph which has inaugurated this introductory discussion, the ensuing pages shall draw out the course of those tears who run along the rusty tracks of the inter-American train-world.

---

7    Even though Cohen (1981) has traced the origins of the song to the 1920s and as part of the culture of black gospel music in the United States, it was Sister Rosetta Tharpe and her diverse recordings of the piece ("This Train", 1939-1943) which popularized the song, which has been covered since then by other performers such as Bob Marley and Johnny Cash. For a study on the train-trope across time and musical genres, see Maxile (2011).

# Laying the Tracks

Picture 1: "Las vías que van al norte, Ixtepec, Oaxaca."
(© Noel Criado, in García Bernal and Núñez Jaime 2011, 154)

In *Memories Have Tongue* (1991), Afua Cooper poetizes individual stories as part of her familial memories. In their particular singularities, these expand however on a collective memory regarding Black diasporic displacement. Referring to stories of mobility across time and space, she poetizes the experience of the Middle Passage in colonial times on the one hand, and later displacement from the Caribbean islands outbound in a neocolonial economy, on the other. In the long prose poem entitled "Roots and Branches", Cooper poetizes her genealogy by referring to how her great-grandparents came from Africa, were forced to resettle in Jamaica as slaves, and whose children and later free grandchildren migrated again, some coming back home only to journey one more time. Such was the case of her Uncle Willie, who "went to work in Panama/ and became an instant celebrity/ upon his return to Jamaica", became more of a personality because of his sojourn in Cuba with the family afterwards, and who wore with style "his Panamanian suit" (Cooper 1992, 25, 21). Together with "My Mother", "My Father's Mother", and "Song of Willie", her poems illustrate how historical memory is collective and yet individual, for both constitute an intertextuality where one is indissoluble of the other (Nora 1989; Halbwachs 1967). Elegantly put, "individual memory is but an enclave of collective memory" (Ricoeur 2000).[8] Her personal story as a Toronto-based Jamaican poet is thus deployed in the form of *roots* that extend in various directions through multiple networks of *branches* that create inevitably a cross-cultural Afro-Caribbean historical imagination in the form of roots and routes (cf. Glissant 1999, 66f.; Gilroy 1995).

Like Cooper, Afro-Panamian writer and sociologist Carlos "Cubena" Guillermo Wilson recreates a story of Caribbean roots re-routed in Central America by installing a narrative dialogue between fictional stories and factual historical data in *Chombo* (1981). A novel that brings to the fore stories like that of Cooper's Uncle Willy, *Chombo* evokes through individual storylines the broader sociohistorical process (*res gestae*) concerning the Afro-Caribbean diaspora in Panama on account of the construction of the Panama Canal. Displacement, mobility, and mooring are in fact at the center of the story's development. In the novel, the Waterloo and Telémaco ships displace people from Caribbean anglophone islands like Jamaica, Barbados, and Trinidad back and forth the *dolorosa cintura de América* (cf. Kohut and Mackenbach 2005). Black contract laborers, as well as their wives, daughters, and granddaughters come and go in search of work as well as of missing family members who emigrated before them with similar – when not exact – purposes. Narrated with a "West Indian Spanish" that code-switches between Spanish and anglophone Caribbean (cf. Smart 1984, 31-50), stories about hope, poverty, and racism as lived by the Black diasporic communities during and after the building of the *Big Ditch* recon-

---

8    "[L]a mémoire individuelle ne serait qu'un rejeton, une enclave, de la mémoire collective." (Ricoeur 2000, 734)

struct the Panama Canal Zone as an enclave territory – one whose descriptions inevitably strike notable parallels with the Central American banana novels, themselves portraits of "banana republics", an expression made popular by the North American writer O. Henry in his short story "The Admiral" (1904, 132). The most noteworthy of these similarities is the representation of the train that cuts across the novels' social landscapes as a "place without a place" (Foucault 1986, 27) connecting locations and people along a map whose routes have been drawn out by power geometries. Scrutinized against the power dynamics latent behind the characters' im/mobile stories, the couple routes/roots acquires hence new meaning. Instead of idealizing nomadism in a globalized order which allows connectivity across circulation, *Chombo*'s social kinetics mirror a dialectics of im/mobilities.

Written in inter-American key, the novel guides the reader across the historical circumstances surrounding the arrival of Black Antilleans in Panama at the beginning of the twentieth century. The novel's plot is deployed across inter-American references that depict the U.S. presence in Panama on the one hand, and the complex enclave dynamics that emerged on account of it on the other. It construes a diasporic bridge between the Caribbean islands and the Central American Caribbean as well, while identifying social conflicts drawn by Caribbean routes/roots in Panama as global experiences shared with other Black communities across the Americas. Cubena does this by connecting oppression and struggle of Black lives in a transnational manner. From segregation and the civil rights movements in the U.S. to Maroon Town in Jamaica, referring also to Martín Fierro in Argentina and the denial of existence of Black people in Mexico, these examples expand on the novel's thematization of the marginalization, invisibility, and erasure of Black agents' contributions to their countries. *Chombo* thus emphasizes how such experiences are not exclusive to Panamanian national/diasporic history, but rather part of a supranational reality concerning Afro-descendants across the globe, what Paul Gilroy re-

ferred to as the *Black Atlantic as a counterculture of Modernity* at
the beginning of the 1990s.

The novel is essentially about volunteer wageworkers who migrated to Panama to build the Canal, hoping to return home once
their work had granted them economic well-being and their contracts had been completed. Caught between the host land and the
desired homeland, return is always at the horizon of *Chombo*'s Car-
ibbean-born characters. Actual displacement back home is neverthe-
less constantly hindered throughout the novel on account of the
characters' social immobility, creating new sites of dwelling. The
disadvantaged position Black people from all over the Caribbean
islands experienced once resettled in Panama is emphasized across
the various singular narratives, as well as the difficulties suffered by
the subsequent Afro-Panamanian generations born out of their original displacement. The novel tells fundamentally of the presence of
a Caribbean diaspora at the Central American isthmus and their difficult integration to the Panamanian democratic nation-state on account of racial considerations of citizenship. The title – "Chombo" –
explicitly underlines this, which is defined in the novel's Glossary
as a derogatory word used in Panama to refer to Afro-Panamanians
of Caribbean origin.[9] Across the novel, the subject of exclusion of
Blacks from the Panamanian imagined community is reiterated and
emphasized thematically as the consequence of racism:

> Me pongo furioso cuando recuerdo todo esto porque, hoy día, a los
> nietos de los que construyen el Canal, que tantos beneficios le da a este
> país, nos insultan gritándonos bembón, pelo cuzcú, ñato, meco, merolo,
> guari-guari, guacuco, yumeca, chombo; [...]. (Cubena 1981, 18)[10]

---

9   "CHOMBO. Nombre despectivo dado al afro-panameño de ascendencia
    antillana." (Cubena 1981, 102)

10  "I get furious when I remember all of this because, still today, the grand-
    children of those who built the Canal, which continues to give so many
    benefits to this country, are offended with racial insults like *bembón,
    pelo cuzcú, ñato, meco, merolo, guari-guari, yumeca, chombo...*". [All
    original literary quotations in Spanish are paraphrased into English by
    the author.]

In this manner, *Chombo* transforms into fiction the failed project of modern democracy in Panama (Pulido Ritter 2013, 33). *Departure* from the Caribbean islands, *arrival* at the Central American Caribbean, and *displacement* across the isthmus and between the continental and insular Caribbean motor the story together with the creation of new sites of mooring. These dialectical movements are meaningful for extracting power dynamics present in the novel's plot since physical movement is narratively aligned to stories of social immobility. While *Chombo* tells of departure, arrival, and settlement of Black Antilleans in what came to be the Panama Canal Zone, these stories of mobility are however associated to the difficult integration of Blacks to Panamanian democracy on account of racism and segregation. By focusing on the literary depiction of the train and of the social world it reenacts, the following pages will approach three individual storylines traversed by the railway system so as to make visible the dialectis of im/mobility that permeate the novel as a whole.

## A Man, A Plan, A Canal

*Chombo* develops along a complex narrative determined by the historical, sociological, and cultural content Cubena incorporates as the factual background to the fictional stories, which are set against the Torrijos-Carter negotiations (1977) regarding the Panama Canal's sovereignty. In so doing, a transgenerational narrative emerges telling of the construction and later functioning of the Panama Canal under North American control as *res gestarum*. In order to accomplish this, the novel's plot does not move chronologically forward in time. The characters' life stories are instead deployed by constant jumps between present and past storylines which intersect one another at strategic moments. Multiple narratives of im/mobility are carefully interlaced across three generations so as to simultaneously frame and deploy the story against a broader sociohistorical process. One that tells of anglophone, francophone, and Spanish-speaking Black Caribbean diasporas and their suffered integration to the Cen-

tral American imagined communities. Accounts of journeys upon
the ship and the train act as narrative nodes across which this is accomplished. Trainscapes become hence meaningful narrative elements since they appear in the novel as the Canal's double, cutting
the storyline transversely.

In Cubena's representation of the Caribbean double diaspora in
Panama (cf. Cohen 1992), ships and the railway system are in fact
the narrative sites that permit the intersection between the fictional
and factual stories being retold. As a consequence, similar narratives
of departure and arrival are read repeatedly yet with historically contingent differences that distinguish the characters' stories meaningfully. This, in turn, regulates the development of the storyline forwards, while parallels between them are deployed. As a consequence, the novel's plot unfolds within what seems to be a cyclical
representation of time, given that the storylines are deployed in diverse time sequences while being structurally similar. The number
*five* is the periodical number that determines this narrative palimp-
sest of cyclical nature which takes place across most part of the
twentieth century, but whose stories can be traced back to the building of the Panamanian Railroad in the nineteenth century.

Though *Chombo* is above all about the Panama Canal and is
considered to be a *novela canalera* (Pulido Ritter 2013), the railway
system is however present as a significant double of the Canal Zone.
The train, together with the Canal, stand as symbols of nineteenth-
and twentieth-century diasporic mobility in the Black circum-
Atlantic.[11] In the novel, the railway system mobilizes people from
one place to another, connecting them from one life to the next. Between multiple plots that develop into palimpsests of im/mobility,

---

11  In order to include regions that Paul Gilroy's "Black Atlantic" has not
    made visible, I opt for the term "Black circum-Atlantic" (cf. Roach
    1996, 5) so as to include regions like the Central American Caribbean to
    the discussion. For as noted by Clifford, "black South America and the
    hybrid Hispanic/black cultures of the Caribbean and Latin America are
    not [...] included in Gilroy's projection. He writes from a North Atlan-
    tic/European location" (1997, 267; cf. Ravasio 2020, 37).

the train is present in the narrative background as a secondary system of mobility. The complex intertwining of spatial and social im/mobility in the Zone are eloquently complemented with diverse trainscapes where individual stories are mobilized and brought to a halt recurrently. Since they do not stand at the spotlight of the story itself and thus lie silent behind the Canal's omnipotence, *Chombo*'s trainscapes resemble rather a ghost that moves about as a symbol of historical imagination. They evoke the fact that the Canal was preceded by the construction of the transisthmian Panama Railroad (1850-1855) – when it was still part of New Granada (now Colombia and Panama) – and underline the entanglement of the Americas across transnational mobile economies.

In *The Path Between the Seas* (1977), David McCullough incorporates the Panama Railroad as part of the Panama Canal's historical "Threshold" (19-44). The California Gold Rush of 1849 had motivated North American entrepreneurs to envision a speedy road that would connect the Pacific to the Atlantic by way of railway tracks, and thus reduce time and distance from and to California. A wealthy private merchant from New York called William Henry Aspinwall began construction of the railroad in 1850 after the Panama Railroad Company came into being on April 13, 1849 (McCullough 1977, 35). The world's first transcontinental railroad was roughly completed five years later as a single-track steamship railway system and was concluded definitely in 1858 (Correa 2015; Maurer and Yu 2001; McCullough 1977). Starting at the Caribbean Limon Bay and finishing at the Bay of Panama on the Pacific seaside, the transisthmian railroad cut across the Panamanian territory "in something over three hours" (McCullough 1977, 35).

Both the construction of the Panama Canal as of the Panama Railroad bear structural similarities concerning the displacement of people on account of transnational and inter-American economic affairs. Something that *Chombo* gives literary form with purposeful verisimilar detail. Like the digging of the Big Ditch, the tracks of the transisthmian iron horse were laid beforehand by foreign hands as well. That is, by a migrant workforce. Representing too high a cost, North American wageworkers were rapidly replaced by Chinese contract labor for the carrying out of the enterprise, of which the vast majority perished (Maurer and Yu 2001, 43f.). As a result, a Caribbean workforce constituted mostly by Jamaicans, together with Irishmen and New Grenadians, would successfully lay the tracks together. Given that the building of the railroad proved to be a challenging task due to environmental and topographical difficulties, most of these migrant workers perished without leaving a trace except as ashes scattered under the railroad lines laid beforehand. It was believed that "there was a dead man for every railroad tie between Colón and Panama City" (McCullough 1977, 36).[12] This reality is not overlooked in *Chombo,* where the narrator underlines in diverse moments of the story how the sweat and blood of Black Antilleans were stolen by the construction of the railroad first, next by the digging of the Big Ditch.[13] Without knowledge of their origins and identities, railroad contract laborers disappeared as collateral damage of the railroad enterprise. Because of their anonymity, their bodies became furthermore "merchandise" for hospitals and medical schools "all over the world" (McCullough 1977, 37), converting the railway system into a site of crucifixion and its victims into human capital.

Opposite this fatal reality, the Panama Railroad represented on the other hand a system of mobility whose modern rapidness and innovative shortening of distances meant capital growth, while developing vast potential for future transnational projects. The railway

12  Except for white employees, no systematic records were kept by the Panama Railroad Company regarding the number of people who died, mostly fallen to tropical diseases like cholera, malaria, smallpox, or fever (McCullough 1977, 37).

13  As for example at the opening pages of the novel: "Además llegué a comprender lo del robo del sudor y la sangre de los negros antillanos durante la construcción del ferrocarril transístimico y la vía interocéanica." ["I also came to understand that the sweat and blood of Black Antilleans had been stolen during the construction of the transisthmian railroad and the interoceanic road."] (Cubena 1981, 18)

system was in fact so crucial to the building of the Panama Canal that the Isthmian Canal Commission invested in repairing and enhancing old tracks, as well as in extending new lines and double-tracking the original ones (Maurer and Yu 2001, 74). In other words, the Panama Railroad helped construct, sustain, and extend the Canal project, becoming vital to it. Against this historical backdrop, the particular trainscapes that are found in *Chombo* correspond to meaningful narrative elements concerning the conformation of the Canal Zone and of the Caribbean communities it mobilized across time. They conjure the past as a shadow of the present.

A couple of decades after the completion of the transisthmian railroad, the French man Ferdinand de Lesseps had managed to consolidate the contract for the building of *La Grande Tranchée* in Panama (1881), which he started a year later with the newly founded *Compagnie universelle du canal interocéanique de Panamá* (Pérez Brignoli 2018, 303). Like with the building of the transisthmian railroad, La Grande Tranchée enterprise contracted once again a Caribbean workforce at the Central American Atlantic seaside, mostly Jamaicans again. Something that had already being set on the move almost a decade earlier (1872) with the construction of the railroad to the Atlantic in Costa Rica (Olien 1977, 139; Chomsky 1996, 24). On account of diverse obstacles like hostile weather conditions, a varied topography, and malaria, the completion of La Grande Tranchée was rendered rather difficult. Unlike his success in the building of the Suez Canal in Egypt (1869), Lessep's project in Panama is known otherwise for its infamous fall into bankruptcy and its relation to the French Panama Scandals in 1889 (Correa 2015, 7). Similar to the railroad project, among the Tranchée's disastrous consequences were once again the high rates of mortality among Caribbean and European workers (Pérez Brignoli 2018, 303). Which is why many of *Chombo*'s characters depart to Panama in the search of their missing relatives, like Afua Cooper's great-uncle "who went/ to help build the Panama Canal and never came back" ("My Father's Mother"; Cooper 1992, 18).

Despite the failed French project, attempts to build a Panama
Canal – an idea already reflected upon by Alexander von Humboldt
in 1811 (Maurer and Yu 2001, 30f.) and allegedly by Abraham Lincoln in the years before his death (Magness and Page 2011, 109-
113; Magness 2008) – were however not relinquished. After military aid was extended by President Roosevelt in 1903, Panama
achieved its independence from New Granada. A strategic move in
geopolitical affairs, this allowed the United States of America to finally sign a Panama Canal Treaty and begin operations in 1904
(Pérez Brignoli 2018, 304). Much like with Lesseps and the building of the railroad beforehand, the Isthmian Canal Commission
turned to low-wage foreign labor for the project, attracting yet again
hundreds of men, women, and children from diverse Caribbean islands. The project was completed in 1914 and became a symbol of
great technological and economic progress in the Americas. Built
and militarized by the United States under the direct control and supervision of President Roosevelt and the Military State Department,
the Panama Canal Zone became consequently a "verdadero enclave
colonial" (Pérez Brignoli 2018, 307f.).

This new form of colonialism in the Americas is depicted in
*Chombo* as none other than displacement of human and material
capital by way of uneven power geometries. Particular trainscapes
are rather revealing of such inter-American dynamics, which deploy
a dialectics of im/mobilities framed against the Canal Zone. An emblematic site characterized by constant movement of people and
things upon the railroad tracks on the one hand, social stagnation for
those people who helped build the Zone complements the narrative
on the other. The troubled integration of Black Antilleans to Panamanian society due to the interlocking of racial and class issues with
notions of belongingness and nationhood constitute in fact the novel's
core theme. This explains the title of the novel and the recurrent
commentaries regarding racism against Black Panamanians of Caribbean origin, such as "todo negro chombo con diploma o sin diploma vale la misma vaina" (Cubena 1981, 77). Moreover, the factual data that gives content to *Chombo*'s fictional stories grant the

novel particular importance. Mainly because the narrative gives voice and grants visibility to the presence of Blacks in Panama by underscoring their importance in the modernization of the country due to the building of the Canal. At the center of the various plots that intertwine with one another and with the broader sociohistorical setting, a complex story of im/mobilities give life to a social world determined by exile, deportation, and unarrival across the Americas.

## Afro-Exile

At the Canal Zone, spatial displacement in the search of work means paradoxically for these mobile people the impossibility to climb up the social ladder. The story of Barbadian James Dunglin provides an emblematic example of this, distinguished by a series of nicknames that define his constant experiences of mobility and standstill across Panamanian territory. His motive force for departure was the disappearance of his father, who had left Barbados upon the Waterloo ship to take part in the building of Lessep's La Grande Tranchée. Once in Panama, the son began looking for his father by working in diverse Big Ditch operations. James became mobile according to jobs, locations, and the possibility of finding his father there, in addition to the higher or lesser degree of mortality that such job opportunities meant for the migrant worker. All these variables become interconnected by way of the railroad tracks and the train gliding upon them, bringing James closer to and simultaneously further away from his return back home.

After taking the Telémaco ship from the insular Caribbean to the Central American Atlantic coast, James rides the train to Gután and then another one to Bas Obispo, hoping to find his father among Barbadians settled there. A literary depiction of an accident that actually took place there in December 1908, a dreadful premature twenty-one tons dynamite explosion killed hundreds of workers by burying them under the gigantic mass of rock (55,000 to 60,000 cubic yards) that piled upon their bodies twenty to thirty feet high (Isthmian Canal Commission 1909, 125). The incident was defined

in *Los Angeles Herald* (1908) as the "most serious accident in con-
nection with the building of the Panama Canal since the United
States took over" (N.A., 1908, 2). In James's storyline, the Bas
Obispo accident is the catalyst event that draws new routes for him.
This time to Culebra, a site just as famous for mortal landslides as
Bas Obispo was for dynamite mortalities. His tale of mobility is
however obstructed here due to sickness. After catching malaria in
Culebra and dwelling in Ancón's hospital, James became the malaria patient of bed number five that refused to die in the hospital
where Blacks never came out alive once they went in (Cubena 1981,
37). This new site of mooring grants him a nickname that discloses
his own personal dialectics of im/mobility, *Cama Cinco*. James's
mobile story is therefore brought to a short-term halt here. His obstruction of movement on account of sickness-caused immobility
takes its toll on his journey and forces him to dwell in horizontality.
The literal reference to his site of dwelling, i.e. *bed n° five*, insinu-
ates horizontal permanence as an obstacle for upward mobility or
physical displacement. His new nickname thus implies how physical immobility inevitably complicates his socioeconomic situation
because of an impossibility to work, interlacing corporeal stoppage
with financial difficulty. For a low-wage immigrant laborer relies on
his bodily strength in order to survive in the enclave economy.

It does not go unnoticed that James's standstill is complemented
by the incorporation of a literary trainscape depicting the five
o'clock train:

> Como la mayor parte de los recursos del hospital se reservaba para los
> pacientes europeos, por desatención muchos de los enfermos negros que
> entraban por la mañana, salían cadáveres por la tarde en rústicos ataúdes
> que eran transportados en el tren de las cinco de la tarde rumbo a las
> fosas comunes." (Cubena 1981, 37)[14]

---

14 "Gven that the majority of the hospital's resources were destined for European patients, due to neglect many of the black sick people that had
been admitted in the morning were discharged as cadavers by the after-
noon in rustic coffins that were transported by the five o'clock train
bound for the mass graves."

This particular *tsc* illustrates a macabre system of mobility which is constituted by inert bodies and exploitative economies that interlace socio-spatial im/mobility in the form of work-related deaths. Numerous dead laborers whose life had been brought to a premature end by train accidents, dynamite explosions, and terminal illnesses at diverse construction sites of the Canal Zone are represented here as traveling to a nameless burial ground. The cadaverous passenger train transports neglected Black bodies from the hospital to mass graves punctually at the hour, deploying a historical imagination that echoes the scenario of the anonymous bodies that disappeared during the laying of the transisthmian tracks, later during La Grande Tranchée's first operations, and now occurring in the Big Ditch reality. James's im/mobile story is unavoidably cut across by the railway system transporting him to his sickness, while incorporating secondary movement towards absolute standstill (i.e. death) as a background setting. In both cases, the trainscape depicts a social world characterized by repetition of unfavorable realities for the Black proletarian diaspora. Nonetheless, reluctant to remain immobile in bed or to lay still in a mass grave, James becomes once again mobile and becomes a successful *pintor de brocha gorda* [house painter] of important buildings and other urbanized spaces of the Canal Zone. It is a matter of time, though, before his story condenses new im/mobilities.

A foreseen return to the homeland was always at the horizon of James's mobile story. As a Barbadian whose reason of travel was first and foremost his father's disappearance, James's desire to return home reinforces his diasporan identity always. It determines his constant displacement across Panamanian territory in order to achieve this, until his return back home is prevented in an absolute manner by third parties who decide over his repatriation. The power exerted upon his displacement back to his place of origin shall determine his social immobility afterwards, developing his im/mobile story into unaccomplished homegoing. Otherwise described as *exile*.

It becomes of upmost interest that Blacks in the Americas are referred to constantly across the novel with the epithet "afro-exiliados". The word is by itself highly representational of the kinetic hierarchies the novel thematizes. On the one hand, exile is but the consequence of forced dislocation on account of third parties that exert power over some social group, for which return to the homeland is hindered. Though the word is used in contexts of political turmoil like dictatorships and civil or world wars, 'exile' comprises in a broad sense the African "victim diaspora" as well (cf. Cohen 2008).[15] For enforced departure and obstructed return movements comprise the foundation of modernity's colonial horizon in the form of the slave trade. Constituted by a coloniality of power (Quijano 2007) which was structured upon the "catastrophic power of race-thinking" (Gilroy 2004, xix), the slave trade meant essentially the impossibility for African slaves and their American-born children to move back to their place of origin after they had been forcefully mobilized away from their homeland. Dwelling in a host land whose social world had been differentiated in hierarchical binaries of metaphysical kind ("superior/inferior", "civilized/barbarian"), the massive mobilization of Blacks slaves signified lastly entrapment within the plantation economies that subjugated their existence and violently hindered their homegoing. The epithet "afro-exiliado" implies this historical backdrop explicitly.[16]

---

15  For Cohen, compulsion and trauma define a 'victim diaspora', which refers to dispersal of a social group to two or more foreign destinations due to a traumatic event in the homeland (2008, 2). The author underscores the particularity of the African victim diaspora by highlighting the "prolonged time scale of the African slave trade" (42).

16  Though Africa has been idealized as an imagined community by Afro-descendants across time and space (Hall 1990, 232), this dialectics of im/mobilities determined ineludibly a gradual erasure of an African collective memory preceding the slave trade (Glissant 1999, 224). So that the epithet 'Afro-exile' implies a metaphorical mobility as well, one that comprises movement away from cultural and historical self-know-ledge prior to the Middle Passage. It evokes hence a complex dialectics of im/mobilities by comprising the impossibility of return both in a corporeal, as in memorial manner. In the hope of curing this traumatic

Itself a novel which undertakes the purpose of thematizing a Black collective memory in Panama as an enclave of the broader Afro-descendant historical imagination, *Chombo* portrays the coloniality of power by thematizing how racial ideology continues to legitimate capitalist relationships and the oppression of the formerly colonized nowadays (cf. Quijano 2007) – specifically in Panama. By coupling "exiliados" with "afro" to refer to the postcolonial Caribbean outcasts of globalized migration in a US-Panamanian neocolonial enclave economy, a link is therefore explicitly traced between social inequalities experienced by Blacks in Panama, and enslaved mobility as the historical origin of their social immobility. The euphemism stands witness to the fact that the "writer sees the situation of the West Indian in Panamá as a case of twentieth century slavery" (Carter 1985, 23), and the Canal Zone as a twentieth-century version of plantation economies (Smart 1984, 81). James's denial of repatriation evokes this.

Repatriation was in fact stipulated in the actual labor contracts that attracted the Caribbean workforce to Panama, both in Lessep's project as in the building of the Canal by U.S. authorities (Maurer and Yu 2011, 78-93). The U.S. first attempted to recruit a Jamaican workforce for Canal operations. This idea was nonetheless abandoned when the Jamaican government, recalling how the crown colony had to pay for repatriation of its subalterns once the French project failed in 1889, demanded the U.S. guarantee repatriation of its workers after the project was completed (79). As a consequence, U.S. authorities turned next to Barbadians, whose malnourishment came at first to little use to their purposes but whose "work ability rapidly improved with access to a complete diet and sufficient calories" provided by Canal authorities (80). Almost twenty thousand Barbadians were recruited by the Canal Commission under labor contracts that offered "a free return trip to Barbados" once their contract expired (91). James himself had a five-hundred-day con-

---

event of forced uprooting, 2019 was announced as the Year of Return by the Ghana government (visit https://repatriatetoghana.com).

tract to complete upon his departure from Barbados, which he over-completed.[17] Yet, even though he had worked more than the time postulated in the original contract, his return homewards was brought to a halt once racism took over such dreams by way of individual hands (Cubena 1981, 46f.).

In a zone described as the "corazón de la discriminación" [the heart of discrimination] (35) and a site of normalized segregation, a former North American employer of James, parodically referred to by the characters and narrator as "Huncle Zam", had kicked his Black employer's head in when he found out he had painted the *Silver Roll* toilet before the *Gold Roll*, as it was accustomed (46). Very much like the Jim Crow system in the United States, the Silver-Gold Roll arrangement of the Canal Zone's social world was too a system of racial segregation in Panama. Not only regarding public spaces, the labor market, and housing arrangements, but also with regards to wages (O'Reggio 2006). Payroll categories were differentiated according to skin color, where black "silver employees" were paid with silver coins, while "gold employees" (mostly North Americans from the south) received gold coins (Guerrón Montero 2014, 29). Though this stratification of labor was supposed to correspond to the skills and capacities of the Canal Zone workers, the Silver-Gold Roll system was in reality "intended to reinforce the concept of inferiority of the Negro" (O'Reggio 2006, 50).

Under the strain of such social and labor dynamics, a Black companion found it but an all-necessary evil to chop off both of Huncle Zam's legs as an act of reparation. As a result, the North American burned all documents with the names of Black Canal workers, among them that of James Dunglin. The forced disappearance of his work records thus hindered his right to repatriation, forcing him to stay in Panama as a modern-day Afro-exile.

---

17   "El había bajado cinco veces la cuota de los quinientos días de labores para tener derecho a repatriación como acordado en el contrato de trabajadores antillanos." ["He had completed five times the five-hundred-day work quota required for repatriation as stipulated in the Antillean laborers' contracts."] (Cubena 1981, 46)

## Tales of Unarrival

James's im/mobile story mirrors transareal mobility on account of capitalist enterprises, yet his narrative is constituted once and again as a story of hindered arrival as well. His narrative is furthermore accompanied by other stories of im/mobility where the aspiration of returning to the homeland is pivotal, as is the story of "a stereotypical grandmother figure" called Nenén (Carter 1985, 22).

The story of Nenén's arrival in Panama starts with the story of Cuffee's departure from Jamaica, her father. Also known as *Kingstonboy*, Cuffee traveled to Panama aboard the same Telémaco ship James was in and with the same intention of finding his missing relatives. Cuffee's grandfather had departed a long time ago to build the transisthmian railroad in Panama, while his father and uncle had drawn out the same route time afterwards to build La Grande Tranchée. His wife decided to part with the purpose of finding the now missing Cuffee, taking with her their only daughter Nenén. Shortly before boarding the Telémaco ship at Kingston's dock, Nenén finds by chance a dying Francis Wilson who had returned from Panama aboard the Telémaco with her newly born daughter. After a five-month intensive search, Francis too had not found her husband George Wilson. Nenén saved the little girl from the dead mother's grip and together, the three searched for Cuffee across Panamanian land upon arrival (Cubena 1981, 40-42).

Like James im/mobile story, Nenén's narratives of im/mobilities are also traversed by the railroad. Once in Colón, the three Jamaican women did not have money to pay for a ride to Ancón, where James and Cuffee had met at the hospital while sick. The interruption of their journey led them to work as maids at a brothel, until the denial of self-prostitution three months into the job made them embark on their search for Cuffee once again. In the following literary trainscape, their social kinetics reveal the complex intertwinement of spatial mobility with social immobility. For given that they are unable to provide economically for mechanized transit, they decide to undertake the difficult task of walking upon the rail-

way lines clandestinely. Nenén's narrative of departure, though put
in motion with the ship, is next complemented by the railway system, which stands as the emblematic site of im/mobility. It provides
first the route towards Cuffee, while simultaneously determining her
mother's end. Due to extreme fatigue, she is brutally run over by the
locomotive and dies upon the railway tracks (43f.). The iron lines
have become yet again a site of death. Nenén and the baby finally
reach the railway station, where their displacement on foot along the
railway tracks finally comes to a complete stop. With time, Nenén
and Amena find a home and a family near the train station with Hai-
tian woman Tidam Frenchí and her child Luisa (44-46). Together,
they shared their suffered existence by mutually supporting themselves.

The train station, which is set against at a busy intersection, es-
tablishes the spatial coordinates for well-being and discord in their
shared storyline. Train-caused mobility is here but a subtle narrative
thread that ties together buyers and vendors, for just around the corner people from different places, languages, nationalities, and ethnicities interact at food stands. The railway station sponsors a dynamic
relationality between immigrants of all sorts, whose interaction is
channeled across economic relationships based on the exchange of
food for money. In fact, the story of the women's economic success
and subsequent failure (52-55) is mapped across the movement that
the busy street witnessed due to the trains that constantly arrived
and departed, sending people to look for something to eat nearby
before, between, and after these moments. While Frenchí worked at
the laundromat, Nenén had a successful cooking business near the
railway station. From *patacones* to *yuca frita, arroz con coco*,
*gingerbeer*, and *guineo*, Nenén sold Caribbean home-cooked food
to transients and workers alike, a business she administered together
with Frenchí. At night, as their bodies rested together after long
hours of hard work, dreams of upward mobility and a return back
home flourished in their chests as the money jar became fuller and
fuller with their hard-earned mutual profits.

Their potential mobilities however are obstructed when a child-ish strife between their daughters led the older women to a heart-felt animosity, one that would not diminish even after the girls made peace. From that day on, their companionship parted ways drastical-ly, and the jar of dreams became gradually emptier as their former customers chose the Italian and Chinese restaurants across the street. This particular trainscape gathers a constellation of immi-grants, since the Greek carpenter and the Hindustani cabinetmaker, together with the French painter and the Galician janitor helped the Italian woman and the Chinese man consolidate their restaurants thanks to Nenén and Frenchí's parting. At that busy intersection near the train station, *Casa Nerón* and *Casa Wong* grew successful-ly with the new customers whose heart had been filled beforehand with warm memories of the distant homeland thanks to Nenén's cooking. The Black clientele helped the Italian woman and the Chi-nese man expand their business to Bella Vista, a high-class neigh-borhood where they opened new restaurants that, ironically, segre-gated and discriminated them.[18]

Contrariwise, the women's Caribbean food business became feebler until it was no longer able to sustain their hopes and dreams. Return movements were interrupted and enrichment, their children's education, and a socioeconomic betterment overall were altogether blocked. Given that Nenén and Frenchí had no more capital to move upwards or away, their dreams halted to a complete stop. Unable to climb the socioeconomic pyramid, they are thus incapable to return home. Like in James's im/mobile story, the representation of the train station stands in the narrative background sustaining these women's dialectics of social and spatial im/mobility. It provides

---

18 "En los nuevos restaurantes de prestigio, para desanimar el patrocinio de negros se les servía pizza fría y sopa wantón tibia. Además, el menú reservado especialmente para negros tenía menos variedad y los precios eran ridículamente elevados." ["At the new prestigious restaurants, in order to discourage black clientele these were served cold pizza and cold wanton soup. Furthermore, the menu which was set-apart for blacks had less variety and the prices were ridiculously high."] (Cubena 1981, 55)

connectivity across the urbanized landscape, routing the social world while the train stands itself in the narrative background as a ghost – silent but present. This literary trainscape also conjures human displacement on the one hand, which gathers and disperses people around Nenén's restaurant, while simultaneously depicting social stagnation and frustrated dreams of homegoing on the other, when strife and competition took over. It is at this location and under these circumstances that James im/mobile story intertwines with Nenén's.

The individual characters' storylines, though heavily determined by disadvantaged socioeconomic conditions, are also orchestrated by counteractive mobilities of ideological kind, as for example concerning James Dunglin's deportation, which appears as the event that follows his denial of repatriation. Forced to stay in Panama after his records were burned, James was later on banished from the Canal Zone because of his relation to the left-wing circles that organized labor strikes. As a consequence, James was deported for life from the Canal Zone (55). Real labor strikes that occurred at the Panama Canal Zone (1919 and 1920) led in fact to the deportation of Afro-Caribbean workers, "their possessions evicted and stacked in the streets" (Maurer and Yu 2011, 81). The novel thus expands on the paradoxical nature of the Canal's kinetic hierarchies by correlating control over spatial mobility by those more powerful, with obstruction of social mobility for those oppressed by the former, mirroring the real world. Both the mobile metaphor of *exile* and of *deportation* exemplify this, highlighting both fictitious and factual power geometries intrinsic to the enclave Zone.

After this forced mobilization, James finds Nenén and Tidam Frenchí and their own im/mobile stories are interlaced with one another, thus producing a broader story of collective im/mobilities. Here, the once malaria-affected Cama Cinco would grow with time new roots as *Papa James*. This new nickname appropriately paints the picture of Dunglin as the paternal figure he came to be for dozens of orphans and disconsolate Antilleans he looked after emotionally and economically during his last years with Nenén after illness, exile, and deportation determined his im/mobile story in Panama.[19] 'Papa James' represents thus another site of mooring regarding his im/mobile storyline, this time in the form of familial roots and branches. James Duglin, a.k.a. Cama Cinco, was finally buried as Papa James once his dreams of homegoing were finally brought to a dead end with a heart attack, much like Nenén's storyline comes to an end after an eye-surgery goes wrong before boarding the ship that would have taken her back home (Cubena 1981, 81-84).

The friction of James's and Nenén's mobility – that is, their gradual slowness until reaching a complete standstill – was determined by dynamic yet contradictory movements. Caught between blocked mobility due to non-repatriation and forced displacement on account of inland enclave-deportation, the host land forced itself on James Dunglin as the new homeland. While Nenén's failed project of upward mobility and the later unaccomplished trip back home defined her mobile story in Panama as one of *unarrival*, caught between her struggles in the host land and the failed return to the homeland. These stories refer mainly to the complex interaction between routes and roots across the insular and continental Caribbean, revealing the historical layers that overlap one another on account of transnational capitalist enterprises in the Americas (i.e. the transisthmian railroad, La Grande Tranchée, and the Big Ditch). These are moreover complemented with the stories of their Afro-Panamanian children.

## Black Panama

In his Preface to *Black Labor in a White Canal* (1985), Michael L. Conniff positively underscores that "the U.S. government ha[d]

---

19   "Para economizar en el pan de cada día, el pintor de Barbados se trasladó al cuarto de Nenén y Abena Mansa Adesimbo. Pero allí los gastos aumentaron cuando fueron a vivir con ellos una docena de huérfanos." ["In order to economize on food costs, the Barbadian painter moved into Nenén's and Abena Mansa Adesimbo's room. But expenses arose when a dozen orphans went to live with them."] (Cubena 1981, 57)

gradually reduced racism and exploitation" and that "descendants of West Indian immigrants [were] treated fairly [...] neither as disadvantaged minority nor as a protected group" (1985, xiii). Published only four years before Conniff's book, Cubena's novel recreates contrariwise the disadvantages, exclusion, and marginalization that Afro-Caribbean immigrants experienced at the Canal Zone due to North American and Panamanian racism during the most part of the twentieth century. If for Conniff the rejection and discrimination of Black immigrants in Panama were in the 1980s "moving in complementary and humane directions" (1985, xiii), Cubena takes pains to make sure the readership undergoes a complex story of Caribbean mobile and immobile subjects whose intertwined lives are determined narratologically by a racist "third-country labor system" (Conniff 1985, xiii). Though Conniff may have had a point at the time regarding how problems of the past had been given a new direction towards a more positive future, experiences of racism, discrimination, and injustice due to racial considerations of national belongingness (i.e. citizenship) constitute the cornerstone of Cubena's novel.

Set in a time frame expanding the most part of the twentieth century, the novel makes purposively visible the long-lasting effects of marginalization and exclusion of Blacks at the Canal Zone as a consequence of U.S. presence. As with the im/mobile stories of James and Nenén, diverse storylines of Caribbean men, women, and children are represented in *Chombo* as unable to accomplish upward mobility despite displacement as transnational wageworkers offering their bodies' strength in exchange of money. The dialectic intersection between physical displacement and social immobility is portrayed across the novel by stressing the existential conditions of Caribbean immigrants and of their offspring in Panama as of detrimental nature. In fact, the Black beggars and scroungers that wander around the railway station evoke this unfavorable reality.[20] They are

---

20  "Cerca de la estación ferroviaria, Lito observó con dolor en el alma a los numerosos mendigos negros que pululaban las sucias calles de Colón. Estos pordioseros, todos afro-exiliados, eran como él descendientes de

described as the abandoned proletariat unashamedly left behind by the failed enterprise of Lessep's La Grande Tranchée once it collapsed towards the end of the nineteenth century.[21] A situation later on repeated by the Big Ditch micro-society that formed around the Canal Zone during the first half of the twentieth century. Once the Canal was finished and started running, the former immigrant workers that helped built it found their place at the lower strata of the socioeconomic hierarchy on account of segregation and racism, while the Canal provided better earnings for the North American economy and its relocated citizens in Panama. Hence, *Chombo* features a poor and decayed cluster of old Antillean men[22] opposite the position of privilege of those at the White Canal Zone.

Antillean Blacks in Panama are thus represented as an underprivileged social group of the Panama Canal Zone. Contrary to Conniff's affirmation, *Chombo* makes a point of how such realities are rather difficult to 'cure' because of their extension in time. Other-

los antillanos que dieron sudor y sangre para construir la lucrativa vía interoceánica." ["Close to the railroad station, Lito observed with a heavy heart the many black beggars that swarmed the dirty streets of Colón. These indigents, all afro-exiles, were like him descendants of the Antilleans that had yielded sweat and blood in order to build the lucrative interoceanic road."] (Cubena 1981, 92)

21   "El joven Duglin buscó por horas, sin éxito, al padre entre la muchedumbre de antillanos que vivían en la más extrema miseria en Colón. En esa época la ciudad atlántica estaba poblada de negros que fueron abandonados allí por la fracasada empresa francesa." ["The young Duglin searched for his father for hours, unsuccessfully, among the multitude of Antilleans that lived in the most extreme poverty in Colón. In that time the Atlantic city was inhabited by blacks that had been abandoned there by the failed French enterprise."] (Cubena 1981, 33)

22   "Además, Nenén a diario, especialmente los domingos, cocinaba como para un ejército e invitaba a comer gratuitamente a muchos desgastados y pobres ancianos que habían trabajado en la construcción del *Big Ditch*." ["Moreover, Nenén cooked daily for an army of people, especially on Sundays, and invited the decayed and poor old men that had worked in the construction of the Big Ditch to eat for free."] (Cubena 1981, 57)

wise put, it would most likely take more time than four short years
to overturn the racist structure deeply embedded in the Canal Zone.
A critical approach to Conniff's affirmation from the perspective of
*Chombo*'s characters and the sociohistorical verisimilitude that deploys their im/mobile stories underscores hence Conniff's perspective as misleading. Nonetheless, it is worth rescuing that Cubena
does not portray solely the story of exclusion and marginalization of
Blacks in Panama. He does this in balance with the social movements that resist and counteract such dynamics of social immobility,
as for example with James's deportation on account of labor unrest,
Nenén's successful cooking business, or with Luisa's storyline, the
daughter of Tidam Frenchí. Her storyline is, in fact, one of upward
mobility, brought to a full circle in the next-to-last chapter entitled
"Kwasiada" (Cubena 1981, 85-96). On the one hand, the literary
trainscape conjures the democratizing, levelling effect the railway
system had for societies on the move. For in the train ride, an array
of people from different origins and nationalities (French, North
American, Afro-Caribbean, Panamanian), as well as ethnicities
(Black, White, Mestizo, Indigenous, Native American, Chicana) are
represented. They are traveling from Río Bajo to Colón for diverse
reasons: as tourists, former missionaries, teachers, students, re-
searchers, and as cooks or soldiers on their way to or from military
bases. Luisa is one of these passengers.

Growing up as a first-generation Afro-Panamanian, the daughter of Tidam Frenchí worked hard to study and become a teacher.
Luisa's right to an education was constantly hindered "since Black
girls were not permitted to attend the public schools" (Carter 1985,
24). She managed however to study by borrowing books from others
and reading at candlelight. Or by eavesdropping school lessons
while standing outside the classroom windows she could not attend.
Later, she would gather the young Black children in her neighbor-
hood so as to teach them the language in which those classes were
taught (Cubena 1981, 52). Though neighbor Fulabuta made fun of
her dream by laughing her head off about it (i.e. "a mandíbula ba-
tiente", Ibid.), Luisa became the teacher that now takes her students

on a class fieldtrip on the train so as to tell them the history of Black Panama. The historical memory she brings to the surface while talking to her students is drawn against a recapitulation of the individual and collective stories that make-up *Chombo*, since many of the characters who emerged in the novel reappear here as passengers, connecting storylines and creating new ones too. This particular trainscape is best described as an individual enclave of the broader plot, where the dialectics between race and nation are transmitted by teacher Luisa.

> ¿Por qué será que en los libros de historia dan tan escasos detalles sobre la gente de ascendencia africana que participó en la fundación de Panamá, la construcción del Ferrocarril, y la excavación del Canal? (Cubena 1981, 16)[23]

While the opening pages of *Chombo* pose the question quoted above regarding why history books withhold almost no references to the mobile Afro-descendants that helped modernize Panama, Luisa's interaction with her young students corrects this silence by teaching them a story of the past which is, in the narrator's words, absent in national history books (88-91). In so doing, it is thematized how Black Panamanians existed simultaneously inside and on the margins of the sociohistorical process leading to the modernization and industrialization of Panama, hence becoming people in but not necessarily part of the nation-state they had migrated to with the hope of fulfilling own dreams of upward mobility (cf. Gilroy 2002, 29). The trainscape thus condenses Chombo's broader storyline, while Luisa embodies the writer's literary and political purpose of revealing the im/mobile story of Afro-Caribbean people in the Canal Zone. This with the purpose of overturning their invisibility in national Panamanian history.

Though exiled into silence, the stories of Antillean im/mobilities are overturned explicitly with this narrative episode, which also

---

23 "Why is it that history books give so scarce details concerning the people of African descent that took part in the foundation of Panama, in the building of the Railroad, and in the excavation of the Canal?"

portrays linguistic borderland dynamics. The *tsc* underlines the fact that different languages are being spoken within a same wagon, so that Spanish, English, code-switching between them, and French color the readers' read along. The trainscape thus performs borderland dynamics quite exemplary by depicting interaction between a heterogenous group of people and *languages* in the travelling train (Cubena 1981, 94f.). Its depiction of plurilingual people in movement is one of its most striking elements withholding historical content regarding the Antillean diaspora in Central America. It depicts the consequences of diasporic departure and subsequent mooring in the form of language contact.

The interaction between three women in the riding wagon – most likely a grandmother, mother, and daughter – mirror the sociolinguistic consequences of an enclave economy. While conversing, the older Antillean grandmother speaks Jamaican English and the mother code-switches between English and Spanish, mirroring her bicultural reality as daughter of the modern double diaspora living in an in-between-place. The youngest of the three, the grandchild of the Antillean woman, dialogues fluently with her grandmother and mother, though she expresses herself solely in Spanish. This literary episode articulates quite elegantly a verisimilar account of the linguistic reality Bryce-Laporte (1962) documented regarding the languages of Afro-Costa Ricans at the second half of the twentieth century (quoted in Herzfeld 1983). The oldest generations of Afro-Costa Ricans spoke English since they were still very much Jamaica-oriented, though they had settled for a long time now in Central America. The following generation expressed itself instead in both English and Spanish, while the youngest one spoke preferably Spanish. This reality was also confirmed by Herzfeld in the 1980s, when she identified Spanish as "the language of prestige" among Afro-Costa Ricans (Herzfeld 1983, 134). She documented how Afro-Costa Ricans perceived it fundamental to their inclusion, both in the political as in the economical domains of the nation-state they had slowly come to belong to. *Chombo*'s trainscape evokes this reality performatively by putting languages in motion while in motion.

The three generations of women described above are confronted by Fulabuta Simeñíquez, a metizo Panamanian woman whose storyline is characterized by extreme racism against Antillean Blacks, especially against Nenén and Tidam Frenchí. She attacks the women's plurilingualism in the train, demanding they speak the language of the nation they inhabit and go back to Africa with their "guariguari" language (Cubena 1981, 94). Although the older woman places her gaze on the floor and remains quiet, the youngest woman confronts Fulabuta by standing up and telling her she is as Panamanian as the national flag, hymn, and flower, and also very proud of her African ascendance (94f.).[24] Her words thus project a sense of empowerment concerning her "pluricentrical belongingness" (Ravasio 2020). That is, a cultural identity that traces connectedness between Africa, the Caribbean archipelago, and the Central American Atlantic territories as a conjunction of multiple cultural and historical foci on account of diasporic displacement. In other words, her words reveal a rhizomatic cultural identity as poeticized in Cooper's "Roots and Branches". In fact, the trifold linguistic repertoire depicted by these women's interaction performs pluricentrical belonging by drawing out linguistic borderlands resulting of human mobilities determined by transnational enclave economies in the Americas, intertwining the U.S., the Caribbean, and Central America. The train becomes here the setting for drawing such connections and historical imaginations where Caribbean routes and Central American roots are condensed into a dialectics of socio-spatial im/mobilities.

---

24 "Yo soy tan panameña como el pabellón tricolor, el Himno Nacional y la flor del Espíritu Santo. Nosotras somos muy orgullosas de nuestra ascendencia africana." (Cubena 1981, 94f.)

# All Aboard?

Picture 2: "Migrante que perdió el tren, San Juan de Ocatán, Jalisco."
(© Héctor Guerrero, in García Bernal and Núñez Jaime 2011, 117)

Around the same time the Panama Canal underwent its first attempt of construction with Lesseps, migrant workers from Italy, China, and the Caribbean were first hired to build the railroad to the Atlantic in the Caribbean province of Limon, Costa Rica. Nonetheless, much like with the building of the Panama Canal, Black hands in their vast majority (Senior 2011, 12) would lay down the tracks under the management of the North American entrepreneur Minor Keith (1848-1929) towards the end of the nineteenth century.

When coffee production peaked in the 1860s, politicians were pressured by the coffee oligarchy to build a port at the Caribbean and an interoceanic railroad connecting inland plantations to it (Olien 1977, 138). Much like the goal behind the Panamanian Railroad was to install a speedy road that would shorten distances from

the Pacific to the Atlantic seaside in the search of El Dorado, the
Costa Rican railroad was also envisioned by liberal politicians so as
to install a faster transit route (Viales Hurtado 2013, 97) from the
inland highlands were coffee was grown, to an Atlantic port that
would mobilize coffee outbound towards Europe and North America. The railway system, thus, signified the modern and industrial
means necessary to "promote the national economy" (Chomsky
1996, 21) by participating in the international market. President José
María Castro Madriz therefore attempted in 1867 to put in motion
the construction of an interoceanic railroad between the Caribbean
port of Limon and the city of Caldera, located in the province of
Puntarenas at the Pacific seaside. Neither General John C. Fremont,
hired for the job by Madriz, nor the North American company contracted by President Jesús Jiménez two years later commenced the
railroad enterprise (Viales Hurtado 2013, 111). The iron road project finally began operations in 1871 thanks to British investment
and the knowledge of Henry Meiggs, the North American magnate
of Andean railroad construction hired by General Tomás Guardia.
Meiggs, in turn, would later on hand the project over to his nephew
Minor Keith.

   In December 1872, the first ship docked in Limon transporting
over hundred migrant workers. In 1874, one thousand Jamaicans,
five hundred Chinese, and another thousand unidentified workers
were working together laying the railroad tracks (Chomsky 1996,
24). Like in the Panama Canal and the Panamanian Railroad beforehand, it was the physical effort of these migrant low-wage workers
that fulfilled the completion of the project. In 1890, only a few decades after the accomplishment of the Panamanian Railroad, tracks
were set between the Central Valley highlands and the Caribbean
province, extending across roughly 160 km of Costa Rican territory
(Viales Hurtado 2013, 111-114).

   At a later time, the same year that La Grande Tranchée declared
bankruptcy, Keith merged his Tropical Trading and Transport Company with the Boston Fruit Company and thus founded the United
Fruit Company in 1899, to which the railway system became fun-

damental. In fact, once his banana enterprise took off, Keith used the existing transport facilities he had himself built as collateral to finance the expansion of his capital across the isthmus (Harpelle 2001). Unlike the building of the Panama Canal, which was a project run by the government of the United States, Minor Keith was a "transnational entrepreneur" (cf. Portes 1996, 3)[25] who operated as a private 'middle-man' between foreign investors (mostly North American and British) and the Central American national governments with the purpose of consolidating his various projects in the region (Quesada Monge 2013, 33-40). By overcapitalizing such projects and thus deferring paying off his debts, Keith was able to reinvest the money so as to expand on his other bigger capitalistic endeavors, like banana production and the railway system. Through this modus operandi, Keith expanded mining, agricultural, electrical, and banking enterprises throughout the region, earning him the title of "the uncrowned King of Central America" (Bitter 1921, quoted in Kepner and Soothill 1976, 44).

This was possible due to the concession leases that the national governments signed with Keith (Quesada Monge 2013, 89). In fact, a decade and a half before the founding of the United Fruit Company, Keith had been granted a 99-year lease to "800,000 acres of undeveloped land along the railroad line" by the Costa Rican government and full undisputed ownership of the railway he was to complete, among other compensations.[26] This corresponded at the

---

25 Portes defines "transnational entrepreneurs" as businessmen whose economic trajectory is one of pronounced ascendency, regulated by the inner laws of the multinational corporations themselves.

26 "The Government grants the Company 800,000 acres of undeveloped national lands along the railroad line or in any other part of the country, to be selected by the company, with all the natural wealth which said areas contain and the strip of land for the right-of-way for the building of the railroad and necessary structures; and all kinds of material necessary for the construction of the railroad which may be found in undeveloped lands anywhere along the railroad; and two of the lots of national property now measured in the port of Limón, for the construction of wharves, warehouses and stations – all without reimbursement of any sort … The

time to almost one-eighth of the country's territory (Rodriguez 2009, 47). Thanks to the Soto-Keith Act, itself a "prototype of subsequent concessions to powerful foreign concerns" in Central America (Kepner and Soothill 1976, 44), Keith was able to overturn the railway's system of mobility at the service of banana export, whose plant he had begun to seed as early as 1878 in order to finance the construction of the railroad in the first place (Rodriguez 2009; Olien 1977). With Costa Rica as the starting point of operations (Rodríguez 2009, 47), Keith thus expanded a *Banana Empire* in neighboring countries (cf. Kepner and Soothill 1976; Ravasio 2020). The railway system became then pivotal in developing a transnational economy across Central America and in conjunction with the U.S. during the first half of the twentieth century, very much like the Panamanian transisthmian railroad became central to the functioning of the Canal. During the years of the Canal construction under U.S. supervision, the neighboring country of Costa Rica lived an economic boom on account of the United Fruit Company (also, UFCo.), whose railway system mobilized its economy, fruit, and *peones*. It is no coincidence that by 1912 Keith controlled the International Railways of Central America (Quesada Monge 2013, 95) together with "transcontinental railroad lines running through Guatemala, Honduras, Nicaragua, Panama, and El Salvador" (Rodriguez 2009, 48).

The implementation of a railroad in Costa Rica at the end of the nineteenth century and the later control of a Central America railway system at the first half of the twentieth century provided not only the infrastructure necessary for expanding a transnational enclave modality of dependent capitalism. It was also responsible for the simultaneous development of new ways of moving, socializing and seeing (cf. Hannam, Sheller, and Urry 2006, 15). During this time, mobilities of people and material goods by the railway system entailed diverse social spaces that were in turn determined by

---

Government cannot lay taxes on said lands within twenty years, counting from the effective date of this concession [...]" (Article XII of the Soto-Keith Act, quoted in Kepner and Soothill 1976, 45).

UFCo. enclave dynamics. Literature had a predominant role in framing the suffered conditions lived at the plantation sites as social testimony thereof. Unlike in *Chombo*, who focuses on the Caribbean double diaspora at the Canal Zone, "Bananos y hombres" (Lyra 2011 [1931]), *Bananos* (Quintana 2002 [1942]), and *Prisión Verde* (Amaya Amador 1957 [1950]) portray another social group whose stories of im/mobility are however also framed by North American transnational enterprises.

These novels sketch inter-American dynamics by depicting a social cartography composed by mestizo workers from all over the region in the form of an *im/mobile peonada*. Though representations of Chinese, Antillean, and autochthonous indigenous people also construe the narratives' social world, these stand rather secondary in the novels' plots, complementing them. Human storylines are developed inside the banana plantations in diverse Central American countries which recreate fictions concerning the struggles of the Central American mestizo proletariat, "product of different labor migrations" (Rodriguez 2009, 53). They mirror the harsh and hostile living conditions that the heterogenous conglomerate of workers on the move suffered on account of enclave social dynamics. The authors' commitment to depict the banana reality from a perspective that put the mobile peón at the focus point reconstructed as a consequence a social world "from below" (Mackenbach 2006). In so doing, the novels explicitly communicate social protest and antiimperialist sentiments regarding the UFCo.'s enterprises in the region, through which the writers "sought to advance a revolutionary agenda in Central America" (Rodriguez 2009, 46).

## Kinetics of Fruit Displacement

In the banana novels, history, ideology, and enclave economies implicate altogether an embodied experience of movement intertwined with death, inequality, and immobility. These novels all depict in one way or another a social world where the dialectics of im/mobility are woven together by the iron machine. As in *Chombo*, the train

is depicted as a double of the enclave economy. Sweeping across
the exuberant nature of the Caribbean plantations, it rides with impetus *under the shadow of the banana* (cf. Putnam 1999, 173) while
framing the characters' im/mobile stories against the endless tracks
of iron. Itself a symbol of progress, freedom, and democracy as syn-
onyms of free circulation, the great iron machine reshaped social
relations in the context of new economic possibilities implied by the
*oro verde*, as referred to in the narratives. Such opportunities are
however portrayed in these novels as failed projects of socioeconomic betterment for those at the bottom of the plantation economy,
who, like the Afro-Caribbeans at the Canal Zone, paradoxically sustain the enclave economy with their own mobile bodies.

In 1931, four years before the national strike against the UFCo.
at the Costa Rican Caribbean Province of Limón, Carmen Lyra published five short stories in the weekly periodical entitled *Repertorio
Americano*, grouped under the title "Bananos y hombres". Portraying grieved existence at the Costa Rican banana enclaves, these stories represent the first prose work regarding Central American antiimperialist literature professed against the United Fruit Company. It
inaugurated the twentieth century banana novel genre, to which
Costa Rican Carlos Luis Fallas's *Mamita Yunai* (1941) and Guatemalan Miguel Angel Asturias' trilogy (1950-1960)[27] are foundational examples thereof. In the banana fields of Lyra's short stories,
women are reduced to sexual partners who bare children who are
never fathered ("Estefanía"). Nature corresponds to a hostile entity
that causes death at the plantation sites in Christmas Eve ("Nochebuena"). Children are portrayed sick and miserable, affected by
their parents' (and own) alcoholism, while the UFCo.'s propaganda
portrays happy, healthy, and smiling children eating Costa Rican
bananas ("Niños"). Lyra's short stories thus paint a critical social
realistic narrative concerning the social world that emerged from the
UFCo.'s presence in the country, intertwining fiction and history
along verisimilar criteria.

---

27   *Viento fuerte* (1950), *El papa verde* (1954), and *Los ojos de los enter-
     rados* (1960).

First published in 1950, Amaya Amador's *Prisión verde* is also
a window into Honduran banana history. A window that frames its
pained breaths caught between life, sickness, and death. The title is
deployed recurrently across the novel as a self-explanatory metaphor. A tripled-faced symbol for the banana enclaves, the color
green remits not only to the foliage of the banana plant and the exuberant environment where it grows, but to the dollar-wealth (i.e. the
green gold) it represented exclusively for the United Fruit Company's magnates and upper commanding strata. Never for the alienated
workforce whose illusions were built on false propaganda, explicitly
criticized by Lyra in "Niños". Moreover, it points to the gridlocked
nature ("prisión") of the banana enclave economy, which was "rooted
in social and economic inequities" (Soluri 2005, 129) that obstructed
the mobile peonada. Existing distraught between the raw fields of
tropical hostility and the money harvested by others from it, the
green prison captured its male, female, and infant inhabitants.

*Bananos*, on the other hand, stories a flow of enclave migrants
that actually *dwell-in-displacement* miserably (cf. Clifford 1992).
Though the subtitle evokes the life of the UFCo. peones ("La vida
de los peones en la yunai"), it is rather ironic given that Quintana
gives literary form to im/mobile stories pertaining to a human caravan he describes as a corpus of *pseudo-men* (2002, 82). Narrating
people in mobility as living cadavers, Emilio Quintana pronounces
the traveling crowd of *Bananos* as an infernal tribulation (8) that
wanders the land opposite the industrialized transit system. A kalei-
doscope of insanitary and dirty perceptions of unbathed and dis-
tressed female travelers give form to Quintana's human caravan together with weeping young boys and moribund beings (6f.).
*Bananos* depicts proletarian mobility as wretched and of a halluci-
natory nature, thus portraying a flow of misery.[28] Quintana's title

---

28   "Pero antes que todo pasó por estos sitios la caravana miserable de la
     peonada alucinada por el halago de un trabajo mejor remunerado." ["The
     miserable peon caravan had passed beforehand through these places, de-
     luded by the flattery of a better paid job."] (Quintana 2002, 12)

mirrors first and foremost the criminal logic of the neocolonial plantation system by writing 'the peón's life' as a *sub*title to *Bananos*.

Carmen Lyra too introduces the reader to "Bananos y hombres" following a similar line of thought. An almighty reign per se, 'bananas' had to be written in the title before 'men' because the export fruit imposed itself ferociously over humans, an entity withholding contrariwise no worth at all (Lyra 2001, 119). The paratextual element can be related to what the banana economy actually accomplished in Costa Rica in the first decade of the twentieth century. Contrary to the 420,000 stems exported in 1884, the U.S. received three million banana bunches in 1900. Two years later, four million. The number more than doubled in 1908 with ten million stems being shipped out from Costa Rica to North America. While just around the corner the Panama Canal was one year short of its inauguration, the United States had become the main consumer of Costa Rican-grown bananas and the small Central American country had thus become the main exporter of bananas at this time.[29] Lyra's introductory paragraph, where she explains the reasons for placing bananas before men in the title, speaks against the intertwinement of U.S. imperialism and banana production on a massive scale because of its disregard for human life, which the author portrays in her short stories.

> Pongo primero BANANOS que HOMBRES porque en las fincas de banano, la fruta ocupa el primer lugar, o más bien el único lugar. En realidad el HOMBRE es una entidad que en esas regiones tiene un valor mínimo y no está en el segundo puesto, sino que en la punta de la cola de los valores que allí se cuentan. (Lyra 2001, 119)[30]

---

29  Data concerning banana exportation in these years can be confronted in Kepner and Soothill 1976, 51f.; Harpelle 2001, 19-25; and Bryce-Laporte and Purcell 1982, 228-230 (cf. Ravasio 2020, 77).

30  "I place BANANA before MEN because in the banana plantations, the fruit occupies first place, or rather the only place. MAN is actually an entity that has in these regions a minimum value and does not hold second place, but instead finds its place at the tail end of the values found there."

Lyra, like Amaya Amador and Quintana, all write vehemently against the paradoxical reality deployed by the green gold. The storylines themselves underscore what the titles imply at a first stance. They describe in vivid detail the disadvantaged position the peonada occupied opposite bananas in the transnational mobile economy.

The main character in these novels is in fact the banana enclave represented in all its authority. Like in *Chombo*'s social world, social cartographies manifest themselves here too as power geometries designed under the shadow of the U.S. umbrella – banana on the one hand, Canal on the other. The literary representations of both enclave economies share not only the human elements of pain, suffering, and death, but more significantly, their trainscapes couple social and spatial mobility narratologically as an inter-American phenomenon. As in *Chombo*, the literary trainscapes depicted in these banana novels reveal the fusion of mobility and immobility by way of a kaleidoscopic reunion of journeys and standstill which moreover mirror the characters' social immobility. They reflect hybrid geographies of bodies-fruit-money dynamics in the form of narratives of captivity, of dwelling-in-displacement, and of mass graves which are set in close relation with unaccomplished dreams of upward mobility. In this manner, an intertextual dialectics of im/mobility intrinsic to the United Fruit Company's train-world can be extracted from Lyra, Quintana, and Amaya Amador's novels. In their singularities, these trainscapes support together the image of being entrapped by 'a colossal, corporate Octopus' (Harpelle 2001, 68; Rodriguez 2009, 48) whose tentacles bestrides the land and souls of the Central American territory across miles and miles of iron tracks. In fact, drawing from the 1926 data, Harpelle documents the UFCo. was present in nine Central American countries at the time and had a contracted force of seventy thousand people. It owned 1,834,000 acres of land it destined for banana, sugar cane, coconut, and cacao production. Furthermore, the UFCo. controlled 1,541 miles of railway and 722 miles of tramways. It owned 187 locomotives, "22 tramtrains, 5,230 railway cars, and 1,859 tramcars"

(2001, 68). Lyra's, Quintana's, and Amaya Amador's trainscapes paint, thus, another picture of the Banana Empire.

The kinetics of fruit displacement and socioeconomic stagnation are well condensed in the novels' trainscapes, framed by a neocolonial inter-American plantation economy that determines the characters' stories of im/mobility. Because "Bananos y hombres" corresponds to a series of short stories, the narratives themselves are perceived as in motion. The individual tales jump from one story to the next composing a variegated portrayal of banana and humans in dynamic relationship with spatial and social im/mobility. Moving from one banana scenery to the next, Lyra's short stories depict journeys of young, sick women and of ill, hurt men displacing themselves on foot, train, motorcars, and boats from the Pacific coast to the Caribbean plantations, back to the capital, and lastly returning to the 'banana' once again. Coupled with stories of poor, illiterate, and unfortunate children, her prose gives life to a social world who moves entrapped between the iron tracks and the banana stems of the "United Banana Co." (Lyra 2001, 126). Though trainscapes are rare and appear randomly, they stand nonetheless as direct references to the UFCo.'s mobile banana economy.

In "Nochebuena", the kinetics of fruit displacement determine the experiences of people in distraught conditions, as well as of those that benefit from their bodily sacrifices. The short story deploys three parallel storylines where stories of well-being and of misery are set against each other. The cargo train cuts across the storyline, interlacing them. While the Costa Rican UFCo. managers enjoy the Christian nativity in a religious, thankful manner, Central American peones stand under heavy tropical showers chopping banana stems. The "preciosa carga" (124) is placed carefully upon the cart that is pulled away by mules, only to be later brought back because of excess fruit in the U.S.' market. This implies in turn the laying off of more banana choppers (125). Just like the peones, motorcar drivers, and banana choppers who celebrate Nochebuena under the torrential deluge that takes over their ranchos violently, the valuable merchandise is discarded and left to rot under the rain on

Christmas Eve. Opposite the peón that hurt his knee while position-
ing the cargo vehicle upon the railroad tracks and who lies now hurt
and immobile on his bed, the North American UFCo.'s assistant
manager, Mr. Sweentums, enjoys his green gold extravagantly in
New York. He has given his girlfriend a Rolls Royce as a Christmas
present. In this storyline, speed, commodity, and wealth are emblematic of displacement of material goods transformed into elite
well-being. While the railway system appears in the narrative to
permit the movement of material goods and thus enrichment for
some, kinetics of fruit displacement by the cargo train directly ob-
struct the peones' well-being. The literary trainscape of this short
story depicts in exemplary fashion the inter-American power geometries intrinsic to the Banana Empire.

Like in Lyra's "Nochebuena", the railway system exists latent
and in the background of Amaya Amador's and Quintana's banana
novels, almost mute if it were not because *tsc* frame the plots' development across im/mobility. Much like a river never abandons its
drift down an endless stream for they are one and the same, indissoluble, the narratives are always somehow accompanied by the
train's presence. In the scenarios of im/mobilities they portray, these
expand on metaphors of socioeconomic exclusion by orchestrating
diverse types of human mobilities according to how the iron machine guides the movement of capital in the Americas. *Motocarros*
but also different kinds of trains (passenger train, cargo train, pay-
train) couple together with the human caravan traversing the mountain by foot, or bodies of water by boat. Trainscapes are thus multifold and not limited to the train but comprise its derived systems of
mobility as well.

It stands out that in *Prisión verde*, on the other hand, *tsc* represent the narrative frame within which the various proletariat stories
are deployed, for Amaya Amador frames his characters' lives and
deaths between them. They cut across the scenery of the *barrancos*
as the intertwining of characters and their life stories emerge, orchestrating their beginning and end. Trainscapes thus represent the
foundational structure sustaining the stories' developments, whose

characters' limits of existence are drawn by the lines of the railway system. Those fixed boundaries of the green prison however dissolve in Emilio Quintana's *Bananos*. Unlike *Prisión Verde*, where the train-world does not stand at the forefront of the story but sustains its limits, Quintana's diegetic narrator is a traveler who hops on and off trains, boats, and *lanchones*, and who furthermore relies on his feet to wander constantly into the mountain in search for new work at diverse Costa Rican banana enclaves. Quintana's train-scapes thus put the narration *in motion*. The novel's core is orchestrated by the train, motorcars and boats, by the human caravan, and by the banana economy who puts all of these elements in movement. *Prisión Verde*, instead, is a novel of immobility and of stillness, of being confined within the bars of a prison whose walls are made of thick undergrowth and green brushwood.

## Reminiscing

*Reminiscing* is a form of travelling to the past that conjures dialectics of im/mobility imaginatively. In *Prisión Verde*, the railroad tracks sustain memory-telling stories that emerge between characters. Walking along iron lines, Máximo Luján tells Martín Samayoa how he came to be a captive of the Honduran green prison. The two men are poor, one unemployed, the other sick because of the job. Samayoa was himself a former land tenant bought off by "la Compañía", now asking Mr. Stills for a job in silent but obvious desperation (Amaya Amador 1957, 11). A captive of the green prison since childhood, Luján reminisces his entrance into the banana world while kilometers ahead follow kilometers left behind (21). On this journey upon gravel and sleeping railroad tracks,[31] Luján shares with Samayoa his narrative of departure.

---

31  "Los dos hombres tomaron hacia occidente caminando sobre los cascajos y 'durmientes' de la vía férrea." ["Both men undertook the voyage west walking upon gravel and sleeping railroad tracks."] (Amaya Amador 1957, 17)

The two men depart from the Compañía's headquarters together and set out on foot to Culuco, a plantation site located rather far away. This narrative episode is literally a walk down memory lane, as Luján tells Martín about his departure from home and into the green prison. His own im/mobile story starts with his father's search of monetary well-being and enrichment by following the green gold. As a child himself, Luján had no choice but to accept his father's plans and flow with him. Nonetheless, unable to settle down in a stable lifestyle, he goes on to explain his fellow travel companion how he wandered with his father from workplace to workplace like "hojas al viento" (18) until he died in a fight. Now in his middle thirties and still unable to break free from the enclave social world, Luján still dwells in displacement because a return home is unimaginable (21). Not because of kinetic hierarchies that exert power over a possible return-movement directly, as in James's denial of repatriation, but because of *captivity*. That is, the banana enclave economy has confined him to an endless job search because he is never able to escape "a cycle of grinding poverty" (Soluri 2005, 129).

The railway lines and the passing cargo train actually frame Lujan's memories of departure and of socio-spatial im/mobility. Before commencing their journey, Luján finds a distraught Samayoa seated in front of the iron tracks (Amaya Amador 1957, 14), whom he explains he will not be able to ride the train since human mobility upon it was prohibited by the Company (16). They then undertake the journey by foot along the railway tracks, where he begins narrating his personal tale. While his im/mobile story unfolds, the image of the railway system accompanies and intercepts his memories of dwelling-in-displacement. Lastly, the train appears afterwards in all of its might so as to close his narrative of departure. This literary trainscape frames thus Lujan's im/mobile story of unfulfilled well-being between the iron tracks and the cargo train that accompany their trip down memory lane as the scenic background. Moreover, his social stagnation is in fact *performed* by the spatial mobility he undertakes with Samayoa, given that while the cargo train rides loudly and with impetus by them, they step aside, then undertake the journey once again. That is, they continue their expedition by foot, sick, and broke, walking along the railway lines instead of riding a train that would shorten the long distance to Culuco and permit the men to arrive faster. The story of their unfavorable socioeconomic condition is thus ironically mirrored by their own capacity to be mobile. Yet this capacity is limited and furthermore restricted by the Company's infrastructure, since the cargo train is for transporting bananas, not peones that harvest those products. The cargo train that interrupts Lujan's personal story makes explicit the kinetic hierarchies that constitute the Company's social world.

As portrayed by this trainscape, the peonada did not have access to speed. Neither upon the freight train nor as motorcar passengers, as the story goes on to narrate further on. The private privilege of speed exemplifies structures of socioeconomic exclusion as intrinsic to the *Prision Verde*'s train-world, as it is implied as well in "Nochebuena" with the Rolls Royce. While the Company's higher strata commanders traversed the same space with greater speed by riding the train and its derivative forms of mobility, the *campeños* Lucio Pardo, Máximo Luján, and Martín Samayoa used their feet to walk to the Company's offices from their barracks at Culuco (44). The novel's kinetics hierarchies are reinforced by the appearance of those that have become recently rich, among them Lupe Sierra, former landlord who had recently sold his lands to the Company. They fly by the campeños in exhilarating speed towards the same destination, travelling upon a motorcar (45). Speed stands opposite the campeños' slowness as an obvious expression of their newly acquired temporary wealth. Sierra and Cantillano's travel on the motorcar to Mister Fox's house reenacts this once more (50f.). It's a matter of time before we encounter these two men again. Not upon the motorcar, but on foot and now asking Mister Fox for work as campeños themselves (134f.). Their story is but an echo of Samayoa's own story of im/mobility. The recurrence of these dialectics of im/mobility underscores the entrapping nature of the Octopus' tentacles.

If *Prisión Verde* is above all a story of departure and non-arrival condensed into *captivity*, *Bananos* paints a *moribund caravan* on endless journey. A reminiscence episode in *Bananos* deploys instead a transnational people on the move. The diegetic narrator rememorates images of his natal Nicaragua when travelling from Puntarenas to the capital of San José upon the Costa Rican train. The view from inside the train does not isolate the narrator from the passing scene that he observes. Instead, the viewer is able to relate to what he is perceiving since he is not alien to it. Distinguishing with his sight a movement of misery propelled by an exploitative economy, the narrator identifies a desolate Costa Rican people similar to the one he had observed while riding a passenger train across Nicaragua. The female vendor crowd, the infant mendicity, and a disillusioned mass of people in distress in both these countries confirmed him that the "trains that travel obliquely across the land are but a reflection of that crazy eagerness to live, otherwise put, of that crazy will to endure the heavy ocean swell bewildered by the economy".[32] The scenery that Quintana's particular trainscape frames here does not represent travel as in *Chombo*'s "Kwasiada", nor as taking part in a privileged context of leisure. Instead, the picture window portrays the dehumanization of its passengers.

Representations of living cadavers, mobility, and standstill are common to banana novel trainscapes, constituting a rail intertextuality. On the one hand, Quintana assimilates the laborers' experience at the Company to a dying body. Either cut in two between the rail lines and the train (10); bit by a *terciopelo* (24); or taken out to the railway to be picked up by the train and transported to the hospital as a remnant of ameba-struck feces (14), Quintana's peonada are reduced to *corpses*. These mentally and bodily 'former-beings' lay exhausted at the mercy of the railway. The green prison is sustained by motorcars and the trains which glide upon the railway tracks transporting cargo similar to how a skeleton structure gives heavy posture to a dying body. Quintana names these "seudohombres"

---

32 "Los trenes que soslayan la tierra son un reflejo de ese loco afán por vivir, por subsistir, mejor dicho, entre el oleaje enloquecido de la economía." (Quintana 2002, 56f.)

(82) while Amaya Amador instead describes them as "subhombres" (1957, 133). Incarcerated within the green prison, the *regadores*, *veneneros*, *chapiadores*, and *corteros* of Culucu's proletariat became also less than human, they became "exhombres" (108). Like Quintana's walking dead and Amaya Amador's non-humans, Lyra too portrays their offspring as living cadavers.

Ranging from toddlers to twelve-year-olds, "Niños" is about infant captivity in the green prison. Ramón and Julia, Anselmo and his four younger siblings, Lidia the young daughter of a prostitute, Martín the motherless child, Natalia and her younger brother are all children of "joyless eyes".[33] Poor, illiterate, unfortunate. These young children exemplify the hostile dialectics of im/mobility contained by the banana enclaves and each infant story is particularly eloquent in exemplifying this. Hoping to help the child accomplish something else in life, Martín's stepmother does laundry for a peón so that he can teach the child to read (Lyra 2001, 130). Natalia's mother, however, must give up on this dream for her daughter since the family moves some six to seven kilometers away. The adults must prepare the mountain for new banana crops (131). In her consideration of children's mobilities with parents, Clare Holdsworth (2014) explains "parents want to maximise the opportunities for their children and will engage in forms of mobility to achieve this" (423). However, adult physical displacement stands here as an obstacle to the child's socioeconomic betterment, since infant illiteracy implies future social immobility for the young girl. The story of Máximo Luján, who wandered away with his father himself still a child, is the living example of such dialectics of im/mobility. Travelling with their parents them too as "leaves in the wind", the children's im/mobile lives are marked by malnourishment, misery, and bodily disease on account of the kinetics of fruit displacement. Like the narrator of *Bananos* attests it, this "childhood is no childhood. It

---

33 "Los niños las contemplan con sus ojos sin alegría." ["The children contemplate them with their joyless eyes."] (Lyra 2001, 131)

is rather innocence raped by humiliation and misery".[34] Accordingly, Máximo Luján from *Prisión Verde* underscores it is not fair to
bear children to the green prison, which will serve, much like themselves, as beasts of burden.[35]

## Open Tombs

The furious tide of this bewildered economy grows with impetus
from the banana plant and falls merciless against the peon and their
offspring, while the soil harvests ramifications of power geometries.
Mobility finds stillness in broken bones and it is in the interspaces
between those fissures where the stories of cadavers unfold. The
soil becomes as such burial ground. Lyra's short stories complement
Quintana's metaphor of *captivity* and Amaya Amador's *moribund
caravan* with depictions of *mass graves* as the site where obstructed
spatial and social mobility intersect. In "Estefanía", it's the sea. In
"Nochebuena", it's the pouring rain and the flooding ranchos. El
Hospital San Juan de Dios at the San José capital represents instead
a third one for the moribund caravan ("Río Arriba"), while in general, and particularly in "Niños", it's the banana plantations in all
their violent authority the mass grave par excellence. Here, the dialectics of im/mobility are crystallized by death, labor mobility, and
unaccomplished dreams.

"Estefanía" corresponds to an imaginative travel brought to life
by the vision of a *cross*.[36] Upon this decolored cross, the name "Estefanía R." can be read. By guessing possible last names for this per-

---

34  "Infancia que no es infancia. Inocencia violada por la humillación y
miseria." (Quintana 2002, 58).

35  "No es justo hacer hijos para que vengan a servir de bestias de carga
como nosotros." (Amaya Amador 1957, 105).

36  "Y una fila de siluetas femeninas [...] comenzó a desfilar por la ima-
ginación [...] Hay una que se destaca [...] El nombre se ha borrado de la
memoria." ["And a row of female silhouettes began strolling the narrator's imagination... There is one that stands out... Her name has been
erased from memory."] (Lyra 2001, 119f.)

son, the testimonial narrator rememorates a woman she once saw travelling with her child. By imagining her tale, the narrator then tells a story of im/mobility about an anonymous dead woman that has being given a name so as to not disappear among many. "Estefanía" stands thus as a synecdoche of the mobile peonada and corresponds to a large degree to a "desconocida". The short story depicts her struggled journey from the Puntarenas province at the Pacific seaside to the Caribbean banana plantations. Later on to the capital's hospital because of banana-caused sickness, and lastly back to the banana province again upon the train and the mule-pulled motorcar transporting cargo. Between these travels, the young twenty-five-year-old Estefanía has given birth to three children from three different men from the capital, jumped from one migrant lover to the next at the banana barracks, and was raped by drunken peones. Her mobile story, as that of her only accompanying daughter, is one of suffered dwelling-in-displacement, which is sustained by the railway system that transports her from one hurt life to the next. Her final standstill, evoked by the decolored cross, does not mean that her displacement through Costa Rica has finally come to a halt. Despite having been buried, the cross appears to have been brought about by the tide. The sea has become "Estefanía's" burial ground.

Crosses and mass graves appear too in *Bananos* as a common narrative thread. Like in "Niños", the banana enclaves themselves represent an archetypal burial ground. Wandering among the dry banana foliage that resembles Hawaiian dancers (Lyra 2001, 123), Quintana's diegetic narrator witnesses how these banana lands are sown with cadavers that have been buried in the jungle.[37] Like it was said regarding mortality and the construction of the Panamanian Railroad, the testimonial narrator from *Bananos* also believes each individual railway sleeper corresponds to a dead man's body.[38]

37 "Toda esta travesía está sembrada de cadáveres." (Quintana 2002, 13)
38 "Por cada polín que sostiene la línea férrea, bien se podría colocar el cadáver de un hombre." ["Every railway sleeper that sustained the iron lines could be easily substituted with a man's cadaver."] (Quintana 2002, 13)

Moreover, the human caravan embodies neither life nor death, but is propelled to wander as an *open tomb* itself.[39] Mobility, death, and exploitation are narratively condensed upon the railroad tracks, when the narrator states that it is along these that peones fall to their death anonymously, very much like those Antillean migrants that built the Panamanian railroad and the Canal. As in "Estefanía", the profane burial of *Banano*'s mobile peonada is signaled by a couple of sticks placed in the form of a cross.[40]

Like in *Chombo*, stories of social immobility in *Prisión Verde* are complemented with social movements that resist and counteract enclave dynamics. Criticizing the government who has handed over the land to foreign concerns by diverse concessions, the peones hold the politicians responsible for their subjugation.[41] Developing class-consciousness, they gather and discuss the establishment of a union in order to demand better working conditions and pay (Amaya Amador 1957, 102). Protesting against hunger and misery, the peones march out of their jobs and strike (109), asking Máximo Luján to be their leader and representative (111f.). At the dawn of the second day, la Compañía's representatives come accompanied by the Coronel and a heavily armed escort, which takes down the social manifestation with armed force and physical violence. While fourteen men are imprisoned and taken away by the cargo train on the next

39 "Todos ellos empujados por el natural derecho de vivir, o mejor dicho de querer vivir muriendo día a día, entre esta desolación que no es vida ni muerte, sino una sepultura abierta [...]" ["All of them pushed on by the natural right to live, or better said, wanting to live while dying day after day, caught between this desolation that is not life nor death, but an open tomb..."] (Quintana 2002, 12).

40 "[...] muchísimos obreros [...] también cayeron a lo largo de esas líneas, ignorados por todos y cuya sepultura quedó señalada por un par de palos clavados en forma de cruz [...]". ["Many workers... also fell along these lines, ignored by all and whose burial was signaled by a pair of sticks anchored into the soil in the form of a cross..."] (Quintana 2002, 10)

41 "'No culpemos tanto a los gringos, sino al gobierno.'" ["Let us not blame so much the gringos (North Americans) as the government."] (Amaya Amador 1957, 121)

day, Máximo Luján instead is separated from the troop and taken away to the railway lines at night (109-118).

If the iron lines first sustained Luján's narrative by rememorating his departure, they become at the end the site where his disappearance occurs. The tracks of iron become thus his *open tomb* after he is murdered by authorities, as implied by the other peones.[42] Lastly, it is precisely on these manipulated tracks that justice and revenge is casted upon with the help of a crashing motorcar, dismembering the bodies held accountable for Luján's disappearance (154f.). His own im/mobile story thus comes to a full circle upon the railway tracks. As in the other novels, the power geometries of the United Fruit Company are condensed here by way of the Central American peones' mobility, exploitation, and death.

---

42  "'¡Si lo habrán asesinado!'" ["They must have murdered him!"] (Amaya Amador 1957, 124).

# Riding the Beast

Picture 3: "A bordo de 'La bestia', Chiapas."
(© Mauricio Palos, in García Bernal and Núñez 2011, 158)

## 72 Migrantes

On August 24, 2010, fifty-eight men and fourteen women were found dead in San Fernando, in the north-eastern department of Tamaulipas located at the border with the United States and the Gulf of Mexico. They were seventy-two people on the move from Ecuador, Honduras, Brasil, and El Salvador in transit through Mexico under irregular conditions. Led by the only identified survivor of the massacre – an eighteen-year old Ecuadorian named Freddy Lala Pomavilla – Mexican marine soldiers found their bodies collapsed on the floor of an abandoned rancho, their eyes blindfolded, and their hands tied. All of them had been executed at point-blank range with the same gun and then placed in an orderly manner against the inside walls of the building. According to the survivor's testimony, who had fled the crime scene with another man after deceiving their perpetrators by pretending they were dead, the criminals – who identified themselves as *Los Zetas* – allegedly killed those seventy-two people because they refused to work for them as hired hitmen. Mexican authorities later confirmed the massacre was carried out by Los Zetas as a message sent out to a rivaling cartel. Former partners in crime, they wanted to send a clear message so as to prevent the others from recruiting hitmen among these mobile migrants (Santamaría 2013, 69). Since the seventy-two migrants refused to work for them, they were immolated (cf. Pérez-Bustillo and Hernández Mares 2016, 122-124).[43]

This massacre in San Fernando has come to represent one of the most dramatic and therefore emblematic incidents of criminal violence against undocumented mobile beings in transit through Mexico. Referred to it as a case of "necropolitan governmentality" (Varela Huerta 2017), the event is emblematic of kinetic hierarchies traversed by the freight train. It exemplifies how the control of people on the move in the country has become now a business organized by drug cartels (Izcara Palacios 2012a, 41).

A compilation of seventy-two photographs and seventy-two short stories, each one written by a different author and corresponding each to a verisimilar account of the seventy-two murdered migrants, the book entitled *72 Migrantes* (García Bernal and Núñez Jaime 2011) portrays too departure and unarrival of mobile beings – this time concerning Central American undocumented migrants.

---

43   The authors draw on the accounts posted on the website https://masde72. periodistasdeapie.org.mx, which was founded by the collective Periodistas de a Pie after the massacre (visited on 27.06.2019). The website contains various official versions communicated to the public concerning the events leading up to the massacre. At the website, the reader can find the official Mexican version delivered by Marine authorities on August 24, 2010, as well as the communication delivered by the U.S. Embassy and disclosed by the National Security Archive (NSA), the results of an investigation as part of a *Licenciatura* thesis, and, lastly, the report elaborated by the Mexican National Commission of Human Rights on the subject (2013).

Published in 2011, *72 Migrantes* (*72M*) was conceptualized firstly in 2010 as a "virtual altar" to commemorate the death and life of these victims, given the absence of a coherent narrative regarding their im/mobile story (Guillermoprieto 2011, 17). Each text is particular. Some of them portray a verisimilar account of an identified migrant, others give a fictional background to bodies that had not yet been identified and later were. While others still lay nameless. A colloquial metaphor used to refer to the freight trains upon which Central American migrants travel 'clandestinely' to the United States across Mexican territory, *La Bestia* is represented across *72M* recurrently. Not only fictionally, but also graphically with insertions of various photographs documenting Central American migrants dwelling in the train's wagons, walking the lines, or riding the train – like the photograph inserted here as an introductory image. In fact, all images included in this study are all portraits taken from *72 Migrantes*.

Text Number "7" (López Collada 2011, 42f.) has a particular narrative form that demands a closer look. The story of departure and unarrival is told in seventy-two single one-word sentences, as the subtitle makes it explicit – "72 palabras". Dedicated to an unidentified victim, this singular story is able to represent the story of the perished group as a whole. Here, the railway system is evoked twice ("tren", "rieles"; 42), while a picture of a young man jumping between La Bestia's wagons color the layout gray. Moreover, the particular spatial distribution of the single-word sentences marcs meaningfully the pauses that determine the reading act. This rhetorical device re-creates the appalling uniqueness of the event. By distributing the last four word-sentences with *spatial* care, the sentiment of dreadfulness that the massacre caused both in Mexico as internationally is summoned aesthetically. Written apart from each other with just enough distance, the concluding words slow down a speed-reading, for the spatial distribution inserts friction. If read aloud, the empty spaces would equal silence. Firstly, because vocal cords and air would stop moving. Mainly, because the blank page forces the reader to focus on the word. Hearing it stand alone in silence, the reader is able to experience the obstruction of movement and the ghastliness of absolute standstill:

Encontrados. Ordenados. Inertes.
Espanto.
Destino.
Mexico.
(López Collada 2011, 43)[44]

A short-story documenting unarrival to the desired destination, the words arranged in the first line of Text 7 align the motive forces with the first steps towards departure: misery and unemployment (42). The act of walking ("Caminata") puts in motion the story. Next, the mobile migrant is blocked before the train ("Inmovilidad. Tren."), then assumes rapid displacement by running and jumping ("Córrele. Bríncale."). Until tripping ("Tropezón") and falling ("Caída"). The first outcome is unarrival in the form of mutilation, abandonment, and death upon the railroad tracks.

Caída. Mutilación. Borbotones. ¡Ayúdenme! Nadie. Vias. Soledad Viento. Lento. Pulso. Luna. Grillos. Desmayo. Muerte. (42)[45]

The second outcome is the massacre.

Approached as the symbol par excellence of departure, journey, and unarrival, La Bestia, a.k.a. *el tren de la muerte*, conjures crucial dimensions of power geometries that emerge around the mobility of the undocumented migrant. Its literary kinetic hierarchies constitute the focus point of the ensuing pages. A detailed hermeneutic of the opening poem of *Libro centroamericano de los muertos* (Balam 2018, 21f.) follows next, which corresponds to an untitled prose poem which stands alone in the section entitled "Sermón del migrante (bajo una ceiba)". The first lines tell of a God in exile which is mi-

44   "Found. Orderly. Inert. Fright. Destiny. Mexico."
45   "Fall. Mutilation. Gushes. ¡Help me! Nobody. Track lines. Loneliness. Wind. Slow. Pulse. Moon. Crickets. Faint. Death."

grating endlessly upon *"La Bestia"* (2018, 21). In this short, yet disturbing literary trainscape, people, goods, and mobility are interlocked by way of the iron horse. It depicts with simple yet cruel imagery a dialectics of im/mobility determined by power geometries which are represented furthermore along a complex poetic narrative. In so doing, the literary dimension artistically re-presents the factual reality that defines La Bestia, for the trainscape expresses exceptionally the ritualized procedure of constant departure and interrupted arrival of Central American undocumented migrants in transit through Mexico.

A land known to be a transit country, Mexico has become a strategic route for those who depart from Nicaragua and the Northern Triangle of Central America (Guatemala, Honduras, El Salvador), as well as from Mexico, South America, the Caribbean islands, and even Asia, with the purpose of entering the United States of America (Casillas 2008, Izcara Palacios 2012a). These mobile beings are referred to as *transmigrants* or *migrants in transit* since their objective after a long and treacherous journey across Mexico is to reach a third country (Anguiano Téllez and Corona Vázquez 2009, 20). That is, to enter the U.S. in order to fulfill their 'American dream'. La Bestia is but one of the various means of transportation used to reach the U.S. border. Because of the overriding power it denotes, the freight trains have become a transcendental symbol of what the dangerous route up North means. The name itself transmits quite an imposing description of it, which indicates a mechanized mobility system of savage nature. The epithet "La Bestia" in fact echoes with accurate precision the description found in *Bananos* decades beforehand regarding the train, i.e. as a black beast of cracking iron and steam.[46]

Although Casillas (2014, 17) has documented that Central American undocumented migrants rely firstly on buses, then on their feet and particular cars, and lastly on the railway system as the

---

46 "[...] una bestia negra con crujidos de hierro y de vapor" (Quintana 2002, 23).

main means of transportation to cross the border, the author's pio-
neer work first documented how the routes of the poorest migrants
were anchored to the railway tracks. The freight train thus had a vital importance in their passage through Mexico (2008, 165). Though
it meant a faster and cheaper way to reach the final destination (Corona, Montenegro, and Serrano 2009, 38), the railway lines however
did not signify a safer transit. Amnesty International (2010) has in
fact described the journey upon La Bestia as one of the most dangerous in the world. Thousands of people riding the Beast not only
face the possibility of mutilation or death because of a fall from the
freight train. They are above all targeted by criminal groups while
on the move, subjected to abuses, abductions, and even murder
(2010, 5).

The trainscape that opens Balam's book reenacts this scenario
in a verisimilar fashion by poeticizing the motive forces that set the
bodies in motion, as well as the challenging experiences they undergo while in movement. The ultimate impossibility of arrival at
the desired destination, on the other hand, motors the literary
trainscape from beginning to end. La Bestia's trainscape is indeed
construed around kaleidoscopic versions of non-arrival, which are
evoked in various textual moments as independent narrative nodes.
As it shall be discussed next, La Bestia's trainscape portrays a dialectics of im/mobility condensed in the story of a God who falls
from the freight train.

### The Falling God

> Y Dios también estaba en exilio, migrando sin término;/ viajaba
> montado en *La Bestia* y no había sufrido crucifixión [...] (lines 1f.;
> Balam 2018, 21)[47]

Though Central American migrants have been transiting Mexico
since the late 1980s, i.e. for at least four decades now, their im/mo-

---

47  "And God was also in exile, migrating endlessly; he was travelling upon
    La Bestia and had not suffered any crucifixion…"

bility has become a special issue of scholarly research, governmental agenda, civil concern, and of diverse NGO organizations since the first decade of the twenty-first century (Martínez, Cobo, and Narváez 2015, 134). Reasons for departure have as a consequence been well documented and have been furthermore acknowledged as a transregional phenomenon. Undocumented migrants that ride the Beast like the poetic falling God have decided to leave their countries due to an array of reasons. Among them are the consequences left behind by civil wars in their countries of origin, gang violence, political conflict, economic struggle, and food insecurity (Rosenblum and Ball 2016). Poverty, for example, constitutes one of the strongest motives for parting. In "Seaworld", the first segment of the short documentary series entitled "Los Invisibles" (Silver and García Bernal 2010), a Honduran woman explains Mexican actor Gael García Bernal the situation in her country is detrimental. Sitting upon railway lines, she shares with him the reasons for her exodus. No job opportunities, daily expenses, and hardly no money to cover basic costs like education supplies for her children were the push factors that led her to undertake the Central American route towards the U.S. (Silver and García Bernal 2010).[48] It does not go unnoticed that they are sitting upon railway lines. In a straightforward manner, the iron lines and the reality she expresses conjure her dialectics of im/mobility enclosed by the silent, yet loudly pervasive tracks of iron. While conversing here, her testimony of frustrated upward mobility and her decision to become mobile in order to overturn this reality become hence indivisible.

La Bestia's trainscape reenacts this indivisibility regarding social and spatial im/mobility by depicting the im/mobile story of a falling God. The manifold representation of His fall from the freight train conjures exemplary how socio-spatial mobility and standstill are entangled with uneven dimensions of power geometries, performing a particular circulation rhetoric characterized by extreme

---

48 See min. 10:55 onwards at http://www.youtube.com/watch?-v=M4oP _M81Ypy.

violence and murder. The story itself is divided in five narrative nodes. Around them, an im/mobile story develops as a circular tale (*ouroboric*) that refers verisimilarly to the actual movements coupled to La Bestia. This is accomplished across several narratives of im/mobility, including departure, mutilation, and immolation, which are all encompassed by the journey upon the poetic Beast. Diverse scenarios accompany the God 'while falling', while the fall in particular stands as the narrative thread that intertwines them all.

## Crucifixions

La Bestia's trainscape has to do with human stories caught between constant departure and interrupted arrival, abstracted in the figure of the falling God. The God who is in exile, as described in the first line, is portrayed across the poem as a synecdoche of Central American transmigrants, much like Estefanía stands as a synonym of the mobile peonada. The sacred personage is linked to the suffered im/mobilities undocumented people on the move experience, since each of the narrative nodes extends an association between real life-stories and their divine embodiment. The divine figure is therefore explicitly used to refer and thus give a concrete form to the anonymous mass of migrants in transit across Mexico as sacrificed beings.

The story commences on top of the moving freight train, only to immediately depict the fall, which may be eloquently described as a *fall from grace*.

> Y Dios también estaba en exilio, migrando sin término;/ viajaba montado en *La Bestia* y no había sufrido crucifixión/ sino mutilación de piernas, brazos, mudo y cenizo todo Él/ mientras caía en cruz desde lo alto de los cielos,/ arrojado por los malandros desde las negras nubes del tren […] (lines 1-5; Balam 2018, 21).[49]

---

49  "And God was also in exile, migrating endlessly; he was travelling upon La Bestia and had not suffered any crucifixion but rather mutilation of legs, arms, mute and ashes all of Him, while He fell crosswise from the heavens above, thrown down by the thugs through the train's dark clouds."

A sacrificed God appears who does not stand crucified above. Instead He is depicted *while falling* ("mientras caía") from the train, through black clouds of smog and to what later shall be described as numerous deaths and new beginnings. Between the moment when the 'God in exile' rides the Beast and the moment of His falling, there is however no catalyst event that sets the latter in motion. Instead, the God is represented upon the Beast journeying endlessly ("sin término") with a mutilated body. Simultaneously, though, the poem's ubiquitous language portrays him as already falling, which is accomplished with the use of the past tense phrase "mientras caía". This implies that the action has begun in some imprecise time beforehand, thus having no punctual beginning, which is why the God is *already falling* by the third line. The *imperfecto* also suggests the fall has no definite endpoint, which in turn implies that the fall occurs endlessly. The trainscape's main narrative is deployed from here on as a slow and eternal downfall, which is framed by the falling body and the railway tracks that sustain the train's wagons. Between these, distinct im/mobilities are described. The im/mobile story is in fact deployed by the God's fall and the narrative episodes that complement it, which depict various forms of victimization. Crucifixion is coupled to the fall repeatedly across the trainscape, outlining it as a multifaceted martyrdom. Though mutilated and without limbs to stretch out, the first narrative node points to the God's body as falling in the form of a cross. Mutilation corresponds, hence, to His first crucifixion.

Although falling from La Bestia means to a large extent the mutilation of the body caught between the riding wagons and the solid railways, a fall can also mean an untimely end. Nonetheless, the poem does not thematize the God's decisive stoppage of movement in the form of demise due to the fall from La Bestia. Instead, it represents the fall as a consequence of multiple forms of violence experienced along the migrant path, among them murder, disappearance, and extorsion. Blockage of transmigrant mobility is first made explicit in the text by referring to violent rituals that take place between clandestine mobile individuals and the people they encounter throughout their journey. The lyrical I is witness to this, whose testimony corresponds to the second narrative node in which she describes who she saw attacking the falling God. That is, the *coyote*, the policemen, the military, and the *narco*:

> y vi claro cómo sus costillas eran atraversadas/ por la lanza circular de los coyotes, por la culata de los policías,/ por la bayoneta de los militares, por la lengua en extorsión/ de los narcos [...] (lines 7-10; Balam 2018, 21).[50]

Traversing the God's ribs with spears, rifle guns, and deceitful discourses while falling with Him from the train, the depiction of these people's involvement in the fall underscores this is not an accidental plunge. Instead, the trainscape's second narrative node portrays the fall as a coordinated execution on behalf of many. Sketched as a violent act orchestrated by multiple agents enforcing power over His own choice of mobility, the God's fall from La Bestia is here portrayed as an immolation.

The above quoted verses depict a common dynamic carried out on behalf of those who are accomplices to the violence exerted nowadays on the mobile transmigrant. Indeed, coyotes represent the solution to a securer transit against extortion inflicted by customs, migratory, municipal, and federal Mexican authorities (Carrasco González 2013). Coyotes offer a safe passage while in transit through Mexico and later across the border in exchange for money. The cost has been stipulated to have tripled since the 1990s, costing firstly under two hundred dollars and nowadays signifying an insecure investment of over three thousand dollars (Casillas 2008, 173). This increase can be explained on account of corrupt authorities that have imposed a quota themselves on coyotes who cross the border with undocumented migrants, rising from one thousand dollars in 1997 to three thousand by 2001 (Izcara Palacios 2012a, 43f.). Also, "false coyotes" sometimes take advantage of undocumented transmigrants

---

50   "And I saw clearly how his ribs were being pierced by the coyote's circular spear, by the butt of the policemen's guns, by the military's bayonet, by the extorting tongue of the narcos..."

by extorting them and asking their families for ransom; taking their money and abandoning them along the way; or by working together with organized crime (Izcara Palacios 2012a, 54f.). Izcara's work on the perception of coyotes regarding U.S. immigration policies (2012b) reveals interesting inter-American dynamics at both sides of the border, highlighting how the problem does not arise solely in Mexican ground.

In this trainscape, diverse acts of violence performed by a chain of actors – coyotes, local and military authorities, organized crime – are crystallized in the weapons they use to immolate the body, each of them representative of their part in the attack. Round spears project disloyalty as a metaphor for the coyote's two-faced personalities; lower end parts of pistols and bayonets represent the power of the law; and deceiving criminal tongues point poetically to the intricate involvement of all of them in the obstruction of His mobility. Mainly because a drop downwards signifies lastly the interruption of advancement forwards. Their violence conjures altogether the falling God's second crucifixion in the form of a *ritual*. Rather than representing a ceremony which venerates the God Himself and His journey in all its vulnerability, this ritual stands as a gruesome cult that conspires in slaughter precisely because of His defenselessness. Articulated as a complicity of various governmental, civilian, and criminal forces, the lyrical I is witness to La Bestia's kinetic hierarchies.

Inspired by the vision of the orchestrated push, the lyrical I moves then back in time. In this temporal turn backwards, a third literary node is deployed in the form of *reminiscence*, which, similar to Lujan's episode in *Prisión Verde*, introduces a narrative of departure. Bearing witness to the God's pain while falling, the lyrical I remembers the time when He was in Central America and used to preach to the masses. He then cites the God, who in His Sunday lecture urged the masses to leave their family, abandon the maras, violence, hunger and misery, and instead follow Him to the U.S. The real-life scenario pushing transmigrants up North from "la esquina rota del mundo" (line 13; Balam 2018, 21) and towards the Ameri-

can Dream (like the Honduran woman's testimony mentioned earlier) is here given poetic form as a sermon. Hence the title of the
section, "Sermón del migrante" [The Migrant's Sermon]. The factual and the fictional world around La Bestia become thus one and the
same in this trainscape, where the incorporation of motive forces
that mirror real tales of departure adds political, economic, and social meaning to the depiction of the in/mobile God's story. The
God's holy words echo the thread that guides the migrants' pace
from the starting point to a desired endpoint.

> "El que quiera seguirme a Estados Unidos,/ que deje a su familia y
> abandone las maras, la violencia,/ el hambre, la miseria, que olvide
> a los infames/ caciques y oligarcas de Centroamérica, y sígame
> […]" (lines 17-20; Balam 2018, 21).[51]

This narrative of departure simulates with a parodic undertone the
religious renunciation of a past life for the promise of a better future
in a distant place and time on account of mobility. The route under-
taken by the holy Migrant becomes then a metaphor for a spiritual
path on the one hand, and representative of personal sacrifice in the
search of upward mobility, on the other. For sacrifice means none
other than giving up something that is valuable to oneself in order to
help others, much like the Honduran woman decides to leave her
family in order to provide for her children from afar. Unlike
"Estefanía", who takes her child with her, as do most of the adult
peones of "Niños" or as Nenén's mother in *Chombo*, who walks the
railroad lines with her daughter until meeting her unfortunate death.
Nonetheless, by coupling the Migrant's sermon to His image while
falling – already mutilated and immolated – the destination He had
beforehand promised in his lecture is exposed now as an illusory
terminus. Despite the Migrant's encouragement to become physical-
ly mobile in order to overcome socioeconomic obstacles and move
up the social ladder, the God's journey is obstructed a third time.

---

51   "Whoever wants to follow me to the United States, leave her/his family
     and abandon the maras, the violence, the hunger, the misery, forget the
     vile caciques and oligarchs of Central America, and follow me…"

This fourth narrative node names the first site of mooring palpable in the trainscape, which appears here too in the form of *mass graves*. Following the reminiscence of the sermon, the God is once again depicted while falling. This time, however, the afterwards of the imminent collapse is described parallel the fall, springing forwards in time. The narrative node thus couples the fall with burial, made explicit with the mention of "fosas communes" (line 23; Balam 2018, 21). In them, the crucified God lies together with hundreds of anonymous migrants that are assassinated every year in Mexico. They too emerge parallel the iron lines, just like *Chombo*'s Canal workers and the banana proletariat.

> [Y] aún mientras caía, antes de las mutilaciones,/ antes de que lo llevaran al forense hecho pedazos/ para ser enterrado en una fosa común como a cualquier otro/ centroamericano, como a los cientos de migrantes/ que cada año mueren asesinados en México [...] (lines 21-25; Balam 2018, 21).[52]

Assassination of moving bodies placed immobile in mass graves articulates as well La Bestia's dialectics of im/mobility. It is outlined here by the mass graves which represent death as the site of mooring that complements dialectically the journeying Beast. The last rite coupled to the God's fall constitutes hence no memorial service, but rather an absent funeral that goes unannounced – a sacrilegious requiem. No cross has been placed here so as to commemorate these lives, as with Estefanía or *Bananos*' infernal tribulation. In its silent and invisible happening, the mutilated bodies are desecrated. For the taciturnity that the mass graves represent signify lastly the disappearance of moving bodies and the coherent ignorance of their immobile whereabouts. The third crucifixion is synonymous of *vanishment* and reveals the inter-American dynamics that Pérez-Bustillo and Hernández Mares (2016) have pointed out:

---

52 "And still while falling, before the mutilations, before He'd be taken to the coroner torn to pieces to be buried in a mass grave like any other Central American, like the hundreds of migrants that are assassinated in Mexico every year..."

"kidnappings" should in fact be characterized as "forced disappear-
ances" to the extent that they are attributable to the actions or omis-
sions of Mexican state civil, military, and police authorities at all
levels of government (local, state, federal), and to the impact of the
U.S. policy imperatives (and aid) which are indented to compel
Mexico to contain and repress flows of undocumented workers towards the U.S. border." (122)

## *Detainment and Deportation*

Mutilation and murder stand opposite sacrifice and hope as forces
obstructing social and spatial mobility, thus determining a story of
im/mobility where departure is defined by its counterpart. That is,
by unarrival on account of obstruction of mobility. Mainly because
falling from La Bestia can mean the dismemberment of joints which
would impede people to keep on moving, such as the falling God
who in the first lines of the poem is represented without arms and
legs. Or because a murder ritual hinders the possibility of overcom-
ing the journey and thus arriving at the destination point. While the
last rite coupled to the God's fall desecrates His journey by making
it anonymous, representative of a massive movement towards disappearance. Each of these crucifixions is furthermore given a meaningful purposefulness by the liturgical narrative of departure, which
sets the scene for the fall. All of these im/mobile narratives are
staged by the iron Beast.

The poem always comes back to the presence of the railway
system as the site of crucifixion, a depiction that is also present in
*Chombo* and in the banana novels. After the sacrilegious burial, the
train is next described as a modern chariot of steel quadrigas pulling
forwards with impetus along labyrinthic paths and upon the rusted
iron horses that lay side by side. These await patiently for the divine
body that floats graciously and inevitably towards its profane mutilation and later anonymous burial, and whose holy flesh and blood
will dye the earth in a ritualistic fashion. This is ingeniously complemented with the reiteration of the God's figure falling with his
arms and body stretched out like a cross, which corresponds to the
poem's *leitmotif*:

mientras caía con los brazos y las piernas en forma de cruz/, antes
de llegar al suelo, a las vías, antes de cortar Su carne/ las cuadrigas
de acero y los caballos de óxido de *La Bestia*,/ antes de que Su ben-
dita sangre tiñiera las varias coronas de espinas/ que ruedan sobre
los rieles clavados con huesos [...] (lines 26-30; Balam 2018, 21).[53]

The fall as an instance of im/mobility, characterized by mutilation,
murder, and disappearance, is further on completed by mentions of
*detainment* and *deportation*. These are written into the final lines of
the poem as concrete examples of His followers' fears. In this narrative node, it is no longer the lyrical I which recalls the God before
departure. It is instead the Lord himself who remembers a conversa-
tion he had under a kapok tree with Francisco Morazán, as described by the section's subtitle ("bajo una ceiba").[54] The human
exodus that flows from Central America up North as an anonymous
and faceless mass of people is given here another name and concrete form with the historical figure of Morazán, who sustained the
Federal Republic of Central America in the first half of the nineteenth century. His presence as the migrant God's disciple is not at
all gratuitous and stands in the text as a defender of Central American unity (cf. Bardales 1983). At the same time, though, his historical transcendence is neutralized by the unfulfilled arrival that the
God's fall signifies. The dialogue between Morazán and the God
makes evident how mobility and standstill are embedded within the
power geometries that constitute La Bestia's circulation rhetoric,
both poetic and factual.

---

53  "While falling with his arms and legs crosswise, before reaching the
    ground and the tracks, before the steel quadrigas and La Bestia's rust
    horses cut His flesh, before His holy blood could dye the various crowns
    of thorns that roll upon the rails that have been nailed with bones..."
54  "[...] y recordó que Morazán le preguntó una vez,/ mientras yacían bajo
    la sombra de una ceiba [...]" ["And he remembered Morazán had once
    asked him, while they laid under the shadow of a kapok tree..."] (lines
    34f.; Balam 2018, 22).

"Maestro, ¿qué debemos de hacer si nos detienen/ y nos deportan?"
(lines 37f.; Balam 2018, 22)[55]

Morazán asked on behalf of all.

Detainment as it is referred to here by Morazán is linked to the
hindering of the migrants' arrival by powerful third parties such as
the U.S. Department of Homeland Security (DHS), which was
founded in 2003 and comprises migration authorities like the Customs and Border Protection (CBP), the U.S. Citizenship and Immigration Services (USCIS), and the Immigration and Customs En-
forcement agency (ICE; cf. Izcara Palacios 2012b, Gavett 2011).[56] It
is to these authorities that undocumented migrants like those represented by Morazán seek to be invisible in order to avoid being re-
tained. Mainly because these are in charge of deporting detained
migrants back to their place of origin.

The "Zero Tolerance" immigration policy implemented in May
2018 by the DHS and the Justice Department under newly elected
President Trump represents the most recent and aggressive attempt
on behalf of the U.S. government to hinder illegal immigration at
the U.S.-Mexico border. The purpose of the policy was to prosecute
those who crossed the border without legal authorization, thus being
charged with "crimes of illegal entry or reentry". This however led
to the separation of migrant children from their parents upon entrance, placing parents in detention facilities and their children in
shelters while they awaited their legal hearings (Pierce, Bolter, and
Selee 2018, 5). Despite being overruled in June 26th and thus having
a short-lived implementation, over five thousand children (Aguilera
2019) were separated from their parents during this period of time,
who were instead *detained*.

The Zero Tolerance policy stands as a particular landmark regarding the criminalization of illegal immigration in the U.S. Nonetheless, it was after 9/11 and under the Bush administration that efforts to increase Border Security were first crystallized with the

---

55   "Master, what shall we do if we are detained and deported?"
56   Visit https://www.cbp.gov and https://www.uscis.gov.

consolidation of privatized immigrant detention services. In 2005, a partnership between the ICE and the Corrections Corporation of America (CCA) was signed to "secure America's borders and reduce illegal immigration", for which the CCA accepted to manage up to six hundred detainees at a correctional center in Taylor, Texas (CCA 2005).[57] Efforts on behalf of the U.S. government to contain immigration flows are no longer solely concentrated at the border but have expanded since then to the interior of the country, where immigration detention has developed into the fastest growing system of incarceration there (Gavett 2011). Interior detention rates reached their highest peak in 2008 and 2009 (Moinester 2018, 1148), while in 2011 the DHS deported over 390,000 documented and undocumented migrants from the U.S., some of them having at least one US-citizen child (Brabeck, Lykes, and Hunter 2014, 497). Currently, the ICE plans "to use data on migrant children to expand deportation efforts" (Miroff 2019), while in April 2020, thousands of migrants continued to be deported despite the declaration of the global COVID-19 pandemic, some of which proved to be infected with the virus (Dickerson and Semple 2020). Moreover, in May 2020, the United Nations Children's Fund (UNICEF) stated that at least one thousand unaccompanied migrant children have been forcefully returned from the U.S. to Mexico, Guatemala, Honduras, and El Salvador (UNICEF 2020).

Under such legal enforcements, *deportation* becomes then a new condition of mobility. This time however in the opposite direction and towards the starting point. Detainment hence goes hand in hand with expulsion, just like Morazán expresses it to his God. For even if the transmigrant enters the desired land, it does not mean the American Dream has been achieved: enforced mobility can always occur. Which is why, when asked by Morazán what to do after be-

---

57   The CCA represents the country's largest provider of correction and detention management services to government agencies. See the CCA press release at their website: http://www.correctionscorp.com/press-releases/cca-announces-agreement-with-immigration-and-customs-enforcement-for-cca-texas-facility.

ing deported, the fallen God advises his disciple to shake the dust of their feet and depart yet again.

> "Maestro, ¿qué debemos de hacer si nos detienen/ y nos deportan?", a lo que Él respondió: "Deben migrar setenta/ veces siete, y si ellos le piden los dólares y los vuelven a deportar,/ denles todo, la capa, la mochila, la botella de agua, los zapatos,/ y sacudan el polvo de sus pies, y vuelvan a migrar nuevamente/ de Centroamérica y México, sin voltear a ver más nunca, atrás…" (lines 37-42; Balam 2018, 22).[58]

It is worth noting that the text reveals *extortion* as the threshold of deportation, corresponding to the fourth crucifixion. A nameless, yet concrete 'they' is described as those who 'take their dollars', though it is not specified on which side of the border they stand. Even though detainment is feared because of U.S. migration authorities, authorities on the other side of the border are also avoided since they exert corrupt extortions on the mobile person.

It is not unusual that Mexican public officials, in conjunction with other delinquent individuals or collectivities, abuse their position of power and demand payments before allowing undocumented migrants to continue their passage (see Casillas 2008; Amnesty International 2010; Izcara Palacios 2012a; Carrasco González 2013). Which is why the fallen God advices Morazán to give them all: their clothes, their bag, the water bottle, their shoes. His answer transmits a strategy of survival that He shares in the likelihood it will grant them permission to continue their journey. Hopefully forwards, or at least backwards, but above all *to persist in movement*. To remain mobile corresponds in fact to the second place of mooring palpable in La Bestia's *tsc*, which is nonetheless displayed as a macabre form

---

58    "'Master, what shall we do if we are detained and deported?', to which He responded: 'You must migrate seventy times seven, and if they ask for your dollars and deport you again, give them everything, your cape, your bag, the water bottle, your shoes, and shake the dust off your feet, and migrate once again from Central America and Mexico, without turning to look never again, behind…'"

of *dwelling-in-displacement*. Its reason of being is none other than the promise of arrival which is constantly hindered on account of mutilation, murder, detainment, and deportation.

## Ouroboric Im/Mobility

By portraying the motive forces aligned to the representation of the God while falling, departure and unarrival are thus intertwined into a narrative of dialectic im/mobility. The nature of this mobile story is furthermore circular, since an imposed return-movement is resolved by the fallen God's incitation to commence again the journey. As the closing lines of the poem express it: *you must migrate seventy times seven, shake the dust of your feet, and depart again without looking back, never again.* This circulation rhetoric portrays an endless story of ouroboric im/mobility, which is moreover very much attuned to the fact that transmigrants actually "will risk making the journey several times in order to achieve their aim" (Amnesty International 2010, 5). The closing lines thus allude eloquently to a circular experience of im/mobility, since the endpoint becomes the starting point yet again.

The reiteration of the words *'while falling'* ("mientras caía") at strategic moments in the text develops new scenarios which occur parallel the fall and that project diverse im/mobilities each time. Firstly, as what appears to be an accidental plunge, next as an orchestrated push, later as disappearance, and lastly as detainment, deportation, and new departure. Each time the falling God is depicted in a new im/mobile state, the plunge downwards is reenacted *ab origine*. On the other hand, due to the use of the *imperfect* past tense ("caía"), the story of the falling God is perceived as never concluding and transmits the image of a spiraling downwards movement, comprising each of the aforementioned im/mobilities. Lastly, since the God's fall has no beginning nor end, it takes place *in illo absente*. Occurring within an unconcluded past that happens over and over again, the fall condenses a ritual, a religious repetition (*sin término, sin fin*) of treachery and exploitation of those most vulnerable while on the move.

With the use of these poetic and rhetorical elements, the poem accomplishes a complex development of the im/mobile story by intertwining the past, the present, and the future without clear temporal boundaries. The narrative frames locate ubiquitously the afterwards of the imminent collapse – like the sacrilegious burial, the return movement, and new parting movements – together with excerpts into the past, like the remembrance of the Migrant's Sermon and the dialogue with Morazán under the kapok tree. The outcome is the depiction of a circulation rhetoric in the form of endless martyrdom. Abstracted in the figures of the cross, the falling God, and the chain of accomplice actors, La Bestia's trainscape reflects poetically the way power geometries are constructed and entangled across socio-spatial im/mobility.

Against the God's *fall from grace*, then, the journey becomes essentially a story of unarrival, where the God's fall is depicted as the journey itself. Mass graves and hope elucidate complementarily the literary *tsc*'s dialectics of im/mobility. They deliver a literary frame where the motives, the routes, the experiences, and the ambiguous endpoint of im/mobile undocumented transmigrants are constructed specifically around the freight train, but mainly as part of a dialectics of im/mobility determined by power geometries and kinetic hierarchies in Mexican territory and in conjunction with the U.S. These re-present a macabre, factual reality that relies on an inhumane inter-American economy. That is, on human capital from the Americas. Throughout the trainscape's deployment of the falling God, the distinction between people and material goods is blurred to the point that they have become one and the same thing. In an implicit manner, the text speaks of *inanimate* merchandise, given that La Bestia is first and foremost a freight train. Yet on the other hand, the *tsc* underscores that the most propitious goods being transported by La Bestia correspond to *human beings* – represented here in divine form, executed four times. In other words, undocumented people on the move riding the freight train like the falling God have become merchandise themselves.

## The Dark Side of Migration

The falling God's trainscape is fairly articulate in depicting kinetic hierarchies where complex relations between bodies in transit and control over those mobile bodies determine restriction and hindering of socio-spatial mobility for some, yet criminal enrichment for others. The lyrical text is able to poetically condemn the fact that massive kidnappings of undocumented migrants at the hands of organized crime have become a troublesome issue concerning human rights violations in Mexico since 2007. The Mexican *Comisión Nacional de Derechos Humanos* (CNDH) presented a report of the situation in 2009, pointing out that the most severe kidnappings occurred in states crossed by the freight train lines, not overlooking the fact that the majority of these acts go unpunished (Amnesty International 2010). The mention of mass graves as the final arrival point of the falling God and of thousands of anonymous, assassinated migrants, signals this explicitly. For in their transit from the southern departments of Chiapas, passing by Oaxaca, then Jalisco, and lastly by Sonora towards the U.S. border, undocumented mobile beings have developed thus into 'hunted' beings. They have become economically rewarding as interchangeable – or in the worst-case scenario – disposable income capital for criminal gangs. The case of the San Fernando massacre exemplifies this, crystallized in the virtual and printed edition of *72 Migrantes*.

Observing the migrants' routes, their movements, grouping, and travelling dynamics, organized crime has been able to detect the migrants' vulnerability and thus create profit from them through a delinquent system feeding on practices of clandestine mobility (Casillas 2014, Izcara Palacios 2012a). This has ravished and proven to develop consistently into a rather sophisticated criminal network involving plural actors, agents, and victims – as the trainscape's second crucifixion evokes it. Affirmed by the United Nations Special Relator Dr. Jorge Bustamante regarding human rights violations of mobile Central Americans in Mexico (2009), "transnational migration continues to be a business in Mexico, largely operated by transnational gang networks involved in smuggling and trafficking in persons and drugs, with collaboration of the local, municipal, state and federal authorities" (quoted in Amnesty International 2010, 12). Amnesty International corroborates this claim and demands that the Mexican government implement adequate control to overturn the situation. The Inter-American Commission of Human Rights (2010) has also denounced the systematic kidnapping and trafficking of undocumented mobile people, concluding that such a large-scale of mass kidnappings occurs fundamentally because of the complicity on behalf of authorities and due to a restrictive migration policy that closes its eyes to human rights violations (Palacios 2011, 25). As asserted by Pérez-Bustillo and Hernández Mares, "Mexico is the leading case in Latin America of the devastating effects of U.S. policies related to migration, free trade and the so-called 'drug war'" (2016, 118f.). These non-governmental institutions have thus brought to the fore how the corrupting of a complex chain of actors by way of bribery, blackmailing or threatening have made possible the trafficking and extorsion of undocumented migrants by delinquent groups of all sorts with support of authorities that exert power over their mobility (Casillas 2014). As a consequence, the *smuggling* of undocumented migrants in the U.S. with the help of coyotes has been gradually taken over by diverse crime organizations who have taken instead to *trafficking* human beings (cf. Núñez Palacios and Carrasco González 2005, Izcara Palacios 2012a). These organizations have expanded their reach of delinquency by violating mobile people's human rights, consolidating what Rodolfo Casillas has keenly named "the dark side of globalized migration" (2011). The portrayal of an orchestrated immolation and the inclusion of mass graves as instances of the falling God's crucifixions poetizes this dark side of migration exemplary.

Nowadays, a series of mixed and alternatives routes have emerged across Mexico that not necessarily follow the railway lines, though these continue to be important to the journey (Martínez, Cobo, and Narváez 2015). The old routes have been creatively transformed according to the risks the journey up North has come to entail and as strategic ways of survival (Casillas 2008). La Bestia's *tsc* is able to summon this historical imagination, which corresponds however to a prevailing and contemporary problematic. In its literary dimension, the *tsc* anchors the representation of material and human capital in a complex atemporal narrative where control over humans' im/mobility becomes a positive investment for some, while a disadvantageous reality for those on the move. By way of divine synecdoche, the God's fall from La Bestia reveals too how, because of a formal and informal clandestine industry that has emerged as collateral damage to the U.S.' attempt to regulate irregular immigration at the border (Leite and Ramos 2009), Central American mobile transmigrants have inevitably become victims of human rights violations. A hermeneutic of La Bestia's trainscape therefore discloses why the exiled God is depicted as falling gracefully to His death from the freight train, for these assaults occur in a *godless* land that stretches parallel the railway tracks along hundreds of kilometers.

# Coda

Picture 4: "Cruces en recuerdo de los migrantes muertos, Nogales, Sonora."
(© Toni Arnau / RUIDO foto / Elfaro.net,
in García Bernal and Núñez Jaime 2011, 127)

The im/mobile stories present in *Chombo*, the banana novels, and the poetic version of La Bestia have been explored throughout these pages in close relation with their specific factual backdrops. Though the literary pieces depict diverging trainscapes according to particular geopolitical imaginaries, each narrative portrays in fact how physical displacement correlates to upward mobility inversely. So that a hermeneutic of trainscapes in literature about the Panama Canal, the banana enclaves in Central America, and the human caravan traversing Mexico underscores the dialectics of im/mobility as an inter-American literary phenomenon. However divergent the representation of trainscapes in these literary pieces, their characters share nonetheless a common element. That of *(not) being on the move*. This allows us to perceive thus the entangled Americas by way of differentiated practices of mobility and of the transnational economies that have propelled them. As a result, fragmented, isolated social histories of the Americas come together into a larger framework of structured mobilities, woven together by the train-world.

In this sense, trainscapes represent a socially dynamic geographical trope that discloses the entanglements of the Americas by means of literary intertextualities that portray patterns of economic exploitation and political irregularity across time and space. On the one hand, trainscapes in *Chombo* trace a transareal mobility that necessarily expands on an *outernational*, i.e. on a diasporic perspective concerning the effects of twentieth-century U.S. enterprises in Panama. This viewpoint is complemented on the other hand with the anti-imperialistic stand of the banana novel genre concerning the presence of the United Fruit Company in the region. Both the *tsc* present in *Chombo* and in the banana novels share striking parallels given that they both reflect dialectics of socio-spatial im/mobility caused by U.S. enclave economies in Central America, to which the railway system was fundamental. Nonetheless, Cubena's text reproduces social, political, ethnic, and cultural issues from a spatial and ethnonational identification that contests the marginalization of Central American-born Blacks in Panama. While the representation of the mobile peonada in the banana novels redefined national identity from the perspective of the Central American mestizo working-class and the rural proletariat (Grinberg Pla and Mackenbach 2006). The depiction of La Bestia, instead, refers to contemporary migratory movements traversing Central America and Mexico up North. These echo nonetheless similar dialectics of im/mobility by portraying as well the correlation between departure, displacement, and unarrival with poverty and frustrated dreams of upward mobility. To ride the Beast, however, corresponds to a rite of passage which is rather unique to such dialectics of im/mobility.

Hence, albeit a close reading of the here analyzed literary trainscapes has revealed a substructure of sociohistorical meaning that is particular to the individual storylines and thus to the historical imaginations and the diverse economies they portray, they all depict nonetheless how power geometries at the Panama Canal, across the banana republics, and upon the Beast rely equally on mobile human capital for their capitalistic success. Which is why, when drawing out the narratives' train-world, these literary historical imaginations create together a kaleidoscopic portrayal of the Americas whose overlapping points of intersection are socioeconomic inequality, physical displacement in order to move up the social ladder, and inhumane economies. All of which are indissoluble of the railway system.

In conclusion, this study has strived to demonstrate how literary trainscapes crystallize kinetic hierarchies in which mobile beings represent the foundation of transnational economies in the Americas and, simultaneously, the victims thereof. Be it the five o'clock train hauling Black cadavers out of the hospital in Ancón to the fosas comunes, the crosses signaling the mobile peonada's burial sites along the railway lines, or the mass graves where the mutilated God rests after falling from La Bestia, the literary trainscapes here analyzed deploy, in fact, the dark side of inter-American migration. Three are the mobile metaphors that portray these power geometries: *Afro-exile*, the *moribund human caravan*, and *La Bestia*. To place them in relation with one another, as it has been done in this study, uncovers not only the fact that socioeconomic and historical processes in the Americas are codependent on mobility, but also that these processes extend both *transareally* as *transhistorically* along tracks of iron. Narratives of im/mobility, of dwelling-in-displacement, and of captivity upon and along the railroad lines depict thus the outcasts of modernity in their inglorious journey across the Americas.

# Works Cited

## Primary Literature

Amaya Amador, Ramón. 1957 (1950). *Prisión Verde*. Buenos Aires: Agepe.

Asturias, Miguel. 1950. *Viento fuerte*. Buenos Aires: Editorial Losada.

_____. 1954. *El papa verde*. Buenos Aires: Editorial Losada.

_____. 1960. *Los ojos de los enterrados*. Buenos Aires: Editorial Losada.

Balam, Rodrigo. 2018. *Libro centroamericano de los Muertos*. México: Fondo de Cultura Económica.

Cooper, Afua. 1992. *Memories Have Tongue*. Toronto: Black Women and Women of Colour Press.

Fallas, Carlos Luis. 1941. *Mamita Yunai*. San José: Soley y Valverde.

Lyra, Carmen. 2011 (1931). "Bananos y hombres." In *Narrativa de Carmen Lyra. Relatos escogidos*, ed. Marianela Camacho Alfaro, 119-137. San José: Editorial Costa Rica.

Quintana, Emilio. 2002 (1942). *Bananos. La vida de los peones en la yunai*. Managua: Ediciones Distribuidora Cultural.

Wilson, Carlos Guillermo (Cubena). 1981. *Chombo*. Miami: Ortex.

## Secondary Literature

Adey, Peter, David Bissell, Kevin Hannam, and Mimi Sheller. 2014. "Introduction". In *The Routledge Handbook of Mobilities*, ed. Peter Adey, David Bissell, Kevin Hannam, and Mimi Sheller, 1-20. London/New York: Routledge.

Aguiar, Marian. 2008. "Making Modernity: Inside the Technological Space of the Railway." *Cultural Critique*, no. 68: 66-85.

Aguilera, Jasmine. 2019. "Here's What to Know About the Status of Family Separation at the U.S. Border, Which Isn't Nearly Over." *Time Magazine* online edition, September 21. Retrieved from https://time.com/5678313/trump-administration-family-separation-lawsuits/.

Amnesty International. 2010. *Invisible Victims. Migrants on the Move in Mexico*. London: Amnesty International Publications.

Anderson, Benedict. 1996. *Imagined Communities. Reflections on the Origin and Spread of Nationalism*. London/New York: Verso.

Anguiano Téllez, María Eugenia and Rodolfo Corona Vázquez, ed. 2009. *Flujos migratorios en la frontera Guatemala-México*. Mexico D.F.: Instituto Nacional de Migración, Centro de Estudios Migratorios, El Colegio de la Frontera, DGE Ediciones.

Aristotle. 1965. *The Poetics*. Trans. W. Hamilton Fyfe. London: Heinemann. Retrieved from http://www.perseus.tufts.edu/hopper/text?doc=Perseus:abo:tlg,0086,034:1457b:6&lang=original.

Bardales, Rafael. 1983. *Morazán, defensor de la unión de Centroamérica*. Tegucigalpa: Editorial Universitaria.

Bauman, Zygmunt. 1990. *Modernity and Ambivalence*. Cambridge: Polity.

Bissell, David. 2009. "Moving with Others: The Sociality of the Railway Journey." In *The Cultures of Alternative Mobilities: Routes Less Travelled*, ed. Philipp Vanini, 55-70. Farnham: Ashgate.

_____ and Fuller, Gillian. 2009. "The Revenge of the Still." *M/C Journal. A Journal on Media and Culture* 12, no. 1. Retrieved from http://journal.mediaculture.org.au/index.php/mcjournal/article/view/136%3E/0.

Bitter, Willhelm. 1921. *Die wirtschaftliche Eroberung Mittelamerikas durch den Bananen-Trust. Organisation und imperialis-*

*tische Bedeutung der United Fruit Company*. Braunschweig: Westermann.

Blumenberg, Hans. 2010. *Paradigms for a Metaphorology*. Trans. Robert Savage. Cornell: Cornell University Press.

Brabeck, Kalina M., M. Brynton Lykes, and Christina Hunter. 2014. "The Psychosocial Impact of Detention and Deportation on U.S. Migrant Children and Families." *American Journal of Orthopsychiatry* 84, no. 5: 496-505.

Bryce-Laporte, Roy Simon. 1962. *Social Relations and Cultural Persistence (or change) among Jamaicans in a rural area of Costa Rica*. PhD. Thesis. University of San Juan, Puerto Rico.

_____ and Trevor Purcell. 1982. "A Lesser Known Chapter of the Diaspora: West Indians in Costa Rica, Central America." In *Global Dimensions of the African Diaspora*, ed. Joseph E. Harris, 219-240. Washington D.C.: Harvard University Press.

Bryson, Norman. 2003. "Cultural Studies and Dance History." In *Meaning in Motion: New Cultural Studies of Dance*, ed. Jane Desmond, 55-77. Durham: Duke University Press.

Carrasco González, Gonzalo. 2013. "La migración centroamericana en su tránsito por México hacia los Estados Unidos." *Alegatos. Revista del Departamento de Derecho de la UAM-Azcapotzalco*, no. 83 (January/April): 169-194.

Carter, Sheila. 1985. "Women in Carlos Guillermo Wilson's *Chombo*." *Afro-Hispanic Review* 4, nos. 2-3: 22-28.

Casillas, Rodolfo. 2008. "Las rutas de los centroamericanos por México, un ejercicio de caracterización, actores principales y complejidades." *Migración y desempleo* (first semester 2008): 157-174.

_____. 2011. "The Dark Side of Globalized Migration: The Rise and Peak of Criminal Networks – The Case of Central Americans in Mexico." *Globalization* 28, no. 3: 295-310.

_____. 2014. *Migración centroamericana en tránsito por México hacia Estados Unidos: Diagnóstico y recomendaciones. Hacia una visión integral, regional y de responsabilidad compartida.* México D.F.: Instituto Tecnológico Autónomo de México.

Chomsky, Aviva. 1996. *West Indian Workers and the United Fruit Company in Costa Rica, 1870-1940.* Baton Rouge/London: Louisiana State University Press.

Clifford, James. 1992. "Travelling Cultures." In *Cultural Studies*, ed. Lawrence Grossberg, 96-116. New York: Routledge.

_____. 1997. *Routes. Travel and Translation in the Late Twentieth Century.* Cambridge (MA)/London: Harvard University Press.

Cohen, Norm. 1981. *Long Steel Rail. The Railroad in American Folksong.* Urbana: University of Illinois Press.

Cohen, Robin. 1992. "The Diaspora of a Diaspora: The Case of the Caribbean." *Social Science Information* 31, no. 1: 159-169.

_____. 2008. *Global Diasporas. An Introduction.* London/New York: Routledge.

Conniff, Michael L. 1985. *Black Labor in a White Canal: Panama 1904-1981.* Pittsburgh: University of Pittsburgh Press.

Corona Vázquez, Rodolfo, Jesús Montenegro Herrera and María Arcelia Serrano Vargas. 2009. "Flujos migratorios en la frontera Guatemala-México: una metodología para su observación." In *Flujos migratorios en la frontera Guatemala-México*, ed. María Eugenia Anguiano Téllez and Rodolfo Corona Vazquez, 33-65. Mexico D.F.: Instituto Nacional de Migración, Centro de Estudios Migratorios, El Colegio de la Frontera, DGE Ediciones.

Correa, Juan. 2015."Ferrocarriles y soberanía: el Ferrocarril de Panamá, 1850-1903." *América Latina en la Historia Económica* 22, no. 2 (May-August): 1-13.

Cresswell, Tim. 2006. *On The Move: Mobility in the Modern Western World.* New York/London: Routledge.

_____. 2010. "Towards a politics of mobility." *Environment and Planning D: Society and Space* 28: 17-31.

Dickerson, Caitlin and Kirk Semple. 2020. "U.S. Deported Thousands Amid Covid-19 Outbreak. Some Proved to Be Sick." *The New York Times* online edition, April 18. Retrieved from https://www.nytimes.com/2020/04/18/us/deportations-coronavirus-guatemala.html.

Floyd, Samuel A. Jr. 1993. "Troping the Blues: From Spirituals to the Concert Hall." *Black Music Research Journal* 13, no. 1: 31-51.

Foucault, Michel. 1986. "Of Other Spaces." Trans. Jay Miskowiec. *Diacritics* 16, no.1: 22-27.

García Bernal, Gael and Víctor Núñez Jaime, eds. 2011. *72 Migrantes*. Oaxaca de Juárez: Editorial Almadía.

Gavett, Gretchen. 2011. "Map: The U.S. Immigration Detention Boom." *Frontline* online edition, October 18. Retrieved from https://www.pbs.org/wgbh/frontline/article/map-the-u-s-immigration-detention-boom/.

Gilroy, Paul. 1994. "Diaspora." *Paragraph* 17, no. 3: 207-212.

_____. 1995. "Roots and Routes: Black Identity as an Outernational Project." In *Racial and Ethnic Identity: Psychological Development and Creative Expression*, ed. Herbert W. Harris, Howard C. Blue, and Ezra E.H. Griffith, 15-30. New York/London: Routledge.

_____. 2002. *The Black Atlantic. Modernity and Double Consciousness*. London/New York: Verso.

_____. 2004. "Foreword: Migrancy, Culture, and a New Map of Europe." In *Blackening Europe: The African American Presence*, ed. Heike Raphael-Hernandez, xi-xxii. Hoboken: Taylor and Francis Books.

Glissant, Édouard. 1999. *Caribbean Discourse: Selected Essays*. Trans. Michael Dash. Charlottesville: University of Virginia.

Graham, Maryemma and Wilfried Raussert, eds. 2016. *Mobile and Entangled America(s)*. London/New York: Routledge.

Grinberg Pla, Valeria and Werner Mackenbach. 2006. *"Banana novel revis(it)ed*: etnia, género y espacio en la novela bananera centroamericana. El caso de *Mamita Yunai."* *Iberoamericana* VI, no. 23: 161-176.

Guerrón Montero, Carla. 2014. "Afro-Antillean Presence in the Latin American Melting Pot." In *African Diaspora in the Cultures of Latin America, the Caribbean, and the United States*, ed. Persephone Braham, 29-45. Wilmington: University of Delaware/Rowman & Littlefield.

Guillermoprieto, Alma. 2011. "Introducción." In *72 Migrantes*, ed. Gael García Bernal and Víctor Núñez Jaime, 17-22. Oaxaca de Juárez: Editorial Almadía.

Halbwachs, Maurice. 1967. *La mémoire collective*. Paris: Les Presses universitaires de France.

Hall, Stuart. 1990. "Cultural Identity and Diaspora." In *Identity: Community, Culture, Difference*, ed. Jonathan Rutherford, 222-237. London: Lawrence and Wishart.

Hannam, Kevin, Mimi Sheller, and John Urry. 2006. "Mobilites, Immobilities and Moorings." *Mobilities* 1, no. 1: 1-22.

Harpelle, Ronald. 2001. *The West Indians of Costa Rica. Race, Class, and the Integration of an Ethnic Minority*. Quebec: McGill-Queen's University Press.

Harrington, Ralph. 2000. "The Railway Journey and the Neurosis of Modernity." *Clio medica* 56: 229-259.

Henry, O. 1904. "The Admiral." In *Cabbages and Kings*, 130-143. New York: Doubleday, Page & Company.

Herzfeld, Anita. 1978. "Vida o muerte del criollo limonense." *Revista de Filología y Lingüística de la Universidad de Costa Rica* 4, no. 2: 17-24.

_____. 1983. "The Creoles of Costa Rica and Panama". In *Central American English*, ed. John Holm, 131-156. Heidelberg: Groos.

_____. 1994. "Language and Identity: The Black Minority of Costa Rica". *Revista de Filología y Lingüística de la Universidad de Costa Rica* 20, no. 1: 113-142.

Holdsworth, Clare. 2014. "Child." In *The Routledge Handbook of Mobilities*, ed. Peter Adey, David Bissell, Kevin Hannam, and Mimi Sheller, 421-428. London/New York: Routledge.

Isthmian Canal Commission. 1909. *Canal Record. Volume 2: September 2, 1908 to August 25, 1909*. Mount Hope: Isthmian Canal Commission Printing Office. Retrieved from https://archive.org/details/panamacanalrecor02isth.

Izcara Palacios, Simón. 2012a. "Coyotaje y grupos delictivos en Tamaulipas." *Latin American Research Review* 47, no. 3: 41-61.

_____. 2012b. "Opinión de los polleros tamaulipecos sobre la política migratoria estadounidense." *Migraciones Internacionales* 6, no. 3: 173-204.

Kaltmeier, Olaf. 2019. "General Introduction to the Routledge Handbook to the History and Society of the Americas." In *The Routledge Handbook to the History and Society of the Americas*, ed. Olaf Kaltmeier, Josef Raab, Michael Stewart Foley, Alice Nash, Stefan Rinke, and Mario Rufer, 1-12. Oxford/New York: Routledge.

_____ and Martin Breuer. 2020. "Social Inequality." In *The Routledge Handbook to the Political Economy and Governance of the Americas*, ed. Olaf Kaltmeier, Anne Tittor, Daniel Hawkins, and Eleonora Rohland, 205-220. Oxford/New York: Routledge.

_____, Josef Raab, Michael Stewart Foley, Alice Nash, Stefan Rinke, and Mario Rufer, eds. 2019. *The Routledge Handbook to the History and Society of the Americas*. Oxford/New York: Routledge.

_____, Anne Tittor, Daniel Hawkins, and Eleonora Rohland, eds. 2020. *The Routledge Handbook to the Political Economy and Governance of the Americas*. Oxford/New York: Routledge.

Kaufmann, Vincent, Manfred Max Bergman, and Dominique Joye. 2004. "Motility: Mobility as Capital." *International Journal of Urban and Regional Research* 28, no. 4 (December): 745-756.

Kepner, Charles and Jay Soothill. 1976. *The Banana Empire. A Case Study of Economic Imperialism*. New York: Russell and Russell.

Kohut, Karl and Werner Mackenbach, eds. 2005. *Literaturas centroamericanas hoy. Desde la dolorosa cintura de América*. Frankfurt a.M./Madrid: Iberoamericana.

Leite, Paula, and Luis Felipe Ramos. 2009. "Migrantes devueltos por las autoridades migratorias de Estados Unidos." In *Flujos migratorios en la frontera Guatemala-México*, ed. María Eugenia Anguiano Téllez and Rodolfo Corona Vazquez, 305-332. Mexico D.F.: Instituto Nacional de Migración, Centro de Estudios Migratorios, El Colegio de la Frontera, DGE Ediciones.

López Collada, Alfonso. 2011. "7. Migrante aún no identificado." In *72 Migrantes*, ed. Gael García Bernal and Víctor Núñez Jaime, 42-43. Oaxaca de Juárez: Editorial Almadía.

Luz, Ana. 2006. "Places-in between: The Transit(ional) Locations of Nomadic Narration." In *Place and Location Studies in Environmental Aesthetics and Semiotics*, ed. Eva Näripéa, Virve Sarapik, and Jaak Tomberg, 146-165. Tallin: Paik.

Mackenbach, Werner. 2006. "Banana Novel Revisited: *Mamita Yunai* o los límites de la construcción de la nación desde abajo." *Káñina, Revista de Artes y Letras de la Universidad de Costa Rica* 30, no. 2: 129-138.

Magness, Phillip. 2008. "Benjamin Butler's Colonization Testimony Reevaluated." *Journal of the Abraham Lincoln Association* 29, no. 1: 1-28.

_____ and Page, Sebastian. 2011. *Colonization after Emancipation. Lincoln and the Movement for Black Resettlement.* Columbia and London: University of Missouri Press.

Martínez, Gabriela, Salvador David Cobo and Juan Carlos Narváez. 2015. "Trazando rutas de la migración de tránsito irregular o no documentada por México." *Perfiles latinoamericanos* 23, no. 45: 127-155.

Massey, Doreen. 1993. "Power-geometry and a progressive sense of place." In *Mapping the Futures. Local Cultures, Global Change*, ed. Jon Bird, Barry Curtis, Tim Putham, George Robertson, and Lisa Tickner, 59-69. London: Routledge.

Maurer, Noel and Carlos Yu. 2011. *The Big Ditch: How America Took, Built, Ran, and Ultimately Gave Away the Panama Canal.* Princeton: Princeton University Press.

Maxile, Horace J. Jr. 2011. "Extensions on a Black Musical Tropology: From Trains to the Mothership (and Beyond)." *Journal of Black Studies* 42, n. 2: 593-608.

McCullough, David. 1977. *The Path Between the Seas. The Construction of the Panama Canal 1870-1914.* New York: Simon and Schuster.

Miroff, Nick. 2019. "Under secret Stephen Miller plan, ICE to use data on migrant children to expand on deportation efforts." *The Washington Post* (Immigration) online edition, December 20. Retrieved from https://www.washingtonpost.com/immigration/under-secret-stephen-miller-plan-ice-to-use-data-on-migrant-children-to-expand-deportation-efforts/2019/12/20/36975b34-22a8-11ea-bed5-880264cc91a9_story.html.

Moinester, Margot. 2018. "Beyond the Border and Into the Heartland: Spatial Patterning of U.S. Immigration Detention." *Demography* 55: 1147-1193.

Muñoz Muñoz, Marianela. 2019. "Afrocentroamericaneidades: dislocación del istmo y translocación caribeña y diaspórica." *Estudios* 38 (June-Novemeber): 1-14.

N.A. 1908. "Fourteen Dead and Fifty Injured at Bas Obispo." *Los Angeles Herald* 36, no. 74, December 14. Retrieved from https://cdnc.ucr.edu/?a=d&d=LAH19081214.2.34&e=-------en--20--1--txt-txIN--------1.

Nora, Pierre. 1989. "Between Memory and History: Les Lieux de Mémoire." Trans. Marc Roudebush. *Representations* 26, Special Issue *Memory and Counter-Memory* (Spring): 7-24.

Núñez Palacios, Susana and Gonzalo Carrasco González. 2005. "Tráfico de migrantes indocumentados en la frontera México-Estados Unidos." *Alegatos. Revista del Departamento de Derecho de la UAM-Azcapotzalco*, no. 61 (September-December): 623-646.

O'Reggio, Trevor. 2006. *Between Alienation and Citizenship. The Evolution of Black West Indian Society in Panama 1914-1964.* Lanham: University Press of America.

Olien, Michael D. 1977. "The Adaptation of West Indian Blacks to North American and Hispanic Culture in Costa Rica." In *Old Roots New Lands. Historical and Anthropological Perspectives on Black Experiences in the Americas*, ed. Ann M. Pescatello, 132-156. Westport et al.: Greenwood Press.

Palacios, Elizabeth. 2011. "Las 72 muertes anunciadas". In *72 Migrantes*, ed. Gael García Bernal and Víctor Núñez Jaime, 23-28. Oaxaca de Juárez: Editorial Almadía.

Pérez Brignoli, Héctor. 2018. *Historia global de América Latina del siglo XXI a la independencia.* Madrid: Alianza Editorial.

Pérez-Bustillo, Camilo and Karla Hernández Mares. 2016. *Human Rights, Hegemony, and Utopia in Latin America. Poverty, Forced Migration and Resistance in Mexico.* Leiden/Boston: Koninklijke Brill.

Pierce, Sarah, Jessica Bolter, and Andrew Selee. 2018. *U.S. Immigration Policy under Trump: Deep Changes and Lasting Impacts.* Washington D.C.: Migration Policy Institute.

Portes, Alejandro. 1996. "Global Villagers: The Rise of Transnational Communities." *The American Prospect* 7, no. 25: 1-8.

Pulido Ritter, Luis. 2013. "La 'novela canalera' en Carlos Guillermo 'Cubena' Wilson." *Cuadernos Intercambio* 10.10, no. 11: 31-47.

Putnam, Lara. 1999. "Ideología racial, práctica social y Estado Liberal en Costa Rica." *Revista de Historia de la Universidad Nacional de Costa Rica* 39: 139-186.

Quesada Monge, Rodrigo. 2013. *Keith en Centroamérica. Imperios y empresarios en el siglo XIX*. San José: Editorial Universidad Estatal a Distancia.

Quijano, Aníbal. 2007. "Colonialidad del poder y clasificación social." In *El giro decolonial: reflexiones para una diversidad epistémica más allá del capitalismo global*, ed. Santiago Castro-Gómez and Ramón Grosfoguel, 93–126. Bogotá: Siglo del Hombre.

Raussert, Wilfried. 2014. "Mobilizing 'America/América': Toward Entangled Americas and a Blueprint for Inter-American 'Area Studies.'" *FIAR. Forum for Inter-American Research* 7, no. 3: 59-97.

_____. 2015. "Selected Key Tropes in Inter-American Studies. Ways of Looking at Entangled Americas." In *Key Tropes in Inter-American Studies. Perspectives from the forum for interamerican research (fiar)*, ed. Wilfried Raussert, Brian Rozema, Yolanda Campos and Marius Littschwager, 1-11. Trier: WVT Wissenschaftlicher Verlag / Arizona: Bilingual Press, Editorial Bilingüe.

_____. 2017. "Introduction." In *The Routledge Companion to Inter-American Studies*, ed. Wilfried Raussert, 1-12. London/New York: Routledge.

_____, José Carlos Lozano, Giselle Anatol, Sarah Corona Berkin, and Sebastian Thies, eds. 2019. *The Routledge Companion to*

*Culture and Media of the Americas*. Oxford/New York: Routledge.

Ravasio, Paola. 2020. *Black Costa Rica: Pluricentrical Belongingness in Afra-Costa Rican Poetry*. Würzburg: University of Würzburg.

Ricoeur, Paul. 2000. "L'écriture de l'historie et la répresentation du passé". *Annales. Histoire, Sciences Sociales* 55, no. 4: 731-747.

Roach, Joseph. 1996. *Cities of the Dead. Circum-Atlantic Performance*. New York: Columbia University Press.

Rodríguez, Ana Patricia. 2009. *Dividing the Isthmus. Central American Transnational Histories, Literatures, and Cultures*. Austin: University of Texas Press.

Rosenblum, Marc and Isabell Ball. 2016. *Trends in Unaccompanied Child and Family Migration from Central America*. Washington, D.C.: Migration Policy Institute.

Safran, William. 1991. "Diasporas in Modern Societies: Myths of Homeland and Return". *Diaspora* 1, no. 1: 83-99.

Santamaría, Gema. 2013. "La difusión y contención del crimen organizado en la subregión México-Centroamérica." In *The Criminal Diaspora: The Spread of Transnational Organized Crime and How to Contain Its Expansion*, ed. Juan Carlos Garzón and Eric L. Olson, 59-99. Washington, D.C.: Woodrow Wilson Center.

Schivelbusch, Wolfgang. 2014. *The Railway Journey. The Industrialization of Time and Space in the Nineteenth Century*. Oakland: University of California Press.

Senior, Diana. 2011. *Ciudadanía afrocostarricense. El gran escenario comprendido entre 1927 y 1963*. San Jose: Editorial Universidad Estatal a Distancia.

Sheller, Mimi. 2014. "The New Mobilities Paradigm for a Live Sociology." *Current Sociology Review* 62, no. 6: 789-811.

_____ and John Urry. 2006. "The new mobilities paradigm." *Environment and Planning A* 38: 207-226.

Silver, Marc and Gael García Bernal. 2010. *Los invisibles*. Mexico D.F.: Canana Films. Retrieved from https://www.youtube.com/watch?v=m2JAu0cLEwc.

Skeggs, Beverley. 2004. *Class, Self, Culture*. London: Routledge.

Smart, Ian. 1984. *Central American Writers of West Indian Origin. A New Hispanic Literature*. Washington: Three Continent Press.

Soluri, John. 2005. *Banana Cultures. Agriculture, Consumption, and Environmental Change in Honduras and the United States*. Austin: University of Texas.

Thompson, Peter. 2014. "Railways." In *The Routledge Handbook of Mobilities*, ed. Peter Adey, David Bissell, Kevin Hannam, and Mimi Sheller, 214-224. London/New York: Routledge.

Tsing, Anna. 2002. "The global situation." In *The Anthropology of Globalization: A Reader*, ed. Jonathan Inda and Renato Rosaldo, 453-485. Oxford: Blackwell.

United Nations Children's Fund (UNICEF). 2020. "COVID-19: Dangers mount for migrant children forcibly returned to northern Central America and Mexico during Pandemic." *Unicef.org*, May 21. Retrieved from https://www.unicef.org/press-releases/covid-19-dangers-mount-migrant-children-forcibly-returned-northern-central-america.

Urry, John. 2000. *Sociology Beyond Societies: Mobilities for the Twenty-First Century*. London et al.: Routledge.

Varela Huerta, Amarela. 2017. "Las masacres de migrantes en San Fernando y Cadereyta: dos ejemplos de gubernamentalidad necropolítica." *Iconos*, n° 58. Retrieved from https://www.redalyc.org/jatsRepo/509/50950776006/html/index.html.

Viales Hurtado, Ronny J. 2013. "La segunda colonización de la región Atlántico/Caribe Costarricense. Del siglo XVI hasta la construcción de la red ferroviaria." In *La conformación histó-*

*rica de la región Atlántico/Caribe costarricense: (Re)interpretaciones sobre su trayectoria entre el siglo XVI y XXI*, ed. Ronny Viales, 89-126. San José: Editorial Costa Rica.

# INTER-AMERICAN STUDIES
## Cultures – Societies – History

# ESTUDIOS INTERAMERICANOS
## Culturas – Sociedades – Historia

This interdisciplinary series examines national and transnational issues in the cultures, societies, and histories of the Americas. It creates a forum for a critical academic dialogue between North and South, promoting an inter-American paradigm that shifts the scholarly focus from methodological nationalism to the wider context of the Western Hemisphere.

Vol. 1

Raab, Josef, Sebastian Thies, and Daniela Noll-Opitz, eds. *Screening the Americas: Narration of Nation in Documentary Film / Proyectando las Américas: Narración de la nación en el cine documental.* 2011. 472 pp.

| | | |
|---|---|---|
| WVT Wissenschaftlicher Verlag Trier | ISBN 978-3-86821-331-7 | € 29,50 |
| Bilingual Press / Editorial Bilingüe | ISBN 978-1-931010-83-2 | $ 29.50 |

Vol. 2

Raussert, Wilfried, and Michelle Habell-Pallán, eds. *Cornbread and Cuchifritos: Ethnic Identity Politics, Transnationalization, and Transculturation in American Urban Popular Music.* 2011. 292 pp.

| | | |
|---|---|---|
| WVT Wissenschaftlicher Verlag Trier | ISBN 978-3-86821-265-5 | € 29,50 |
| Bilingual Press / Editorial Bilingüe | ISBN 978- 1-931010-80-1 | $ 29.50 |

Vol. 3

Butler, Martin, Jens Martin Gurr, and Olaf Kaltmeier, eds. *EthniCities: Metropolitan Cultures and Ethnic Identities in the Americas.* 2011. 268 pp.

| | | |
|---|---|---|
| WVT Wissenschaftlicher Verlag Trier | ISBN 978-3-86821-310-2 | € 29,50 |
| Bilingual Press / Editorial Bilingüe | ISBN 978-1-931010-81-8 | $ 29.50 |

Vol. 4

Gurr, Jens Martin, and Wilfried Raussert, eds. *Cityscapes in the Americas and Beyond: Representations of Urban Complexity in Literature and Film.* 2011. 300 pp.

| | | |
|---|---|---|
| WVT Wissenschaftlicher Verlag Trier | ISBN 978-3-86821-324-9 | € 29,50 |
| Bilingual Press / Editorial Bilingüe | ISBN 978-1-931010-82-5 | $ 29.50 |

Vol. 5
Kirschner, Luz Angélica, ed. *Expanding* Latinidad*: An Inter-American Perspective.*
2012. 292 pp.

| | | |
|---|---|---|
| WVT Wissenschaftlicher Verlag Trier | ISBN 978-3-86821-309-6 | € 29,50 |
| Bilingual Press / Editorial Bilingüe | ISBN 978-1-931010-84-9 | $ 29.50 |

Vol. 6
Raussert, Wilfried, and Graciela Martínez-Zalce, eds. *(Re)Discovering 'America': Road Movies and Other Travel Narratives in North America / (Re)Descubriendo 'América': Road movie y otras narrativas de viaje en América del Norte.* 2012. 252 pp.

| | | |
|---|---|---|
| WVT Wissenschaftlicher Verlag Trier | ISBN 978-3-86821-384-3 | € 29,50 |
| Bilingual Press / Editorial Bilingüe | ISBN 978-1-931010-91-7 | $ 29.50 |

Vol. 7
Kaltmeier, Olaf, ed. *Transnational Americas: Envisioning Inter-American Area Studies in Globalization Processes.* 2013. 278 pp.

| | | |
|---|---|---|
| WVT Wissenschaftlicher Verlag Trier | ISBN 978-3-86821-415-4 | € 29,50 |
| Bilingual Press / Editorial Bilingüe | ISBN 978-1-931010-92-4 | $ 29.50 |

Vol. 8
Raab, Josef, and Alexander Greiffenstern, eds. *Interculturalism in North America: Canada, the United States, Mexico, and Beyond.* 2013. 312 pp.

| | | |
|---|---|---|
| WVT Wissenschaftlicher Verlag Trier | ISBN 978-3-86821-460-4 | € 29,50 |
| Bilingual Press / Editorial Bilingüe | ISBN 978-1-931010-99-3 | $ 29.50 |

Vol. 9
Raab, Josef, ed. *New World Colors: Ethnicity, Belonging, and Difference in the Americas.* 2014. 418 pp.

| | | |
|---|---|---|
| WVT Wissenschaftlicher Verlag Trier | ISBN 978-3-86821-461-1 | € 29,50 |
| Bilingual Press / Editorial Bilingüe | ISBN 978-1-939743-00-8 | $ 39.50 |

Vol. 10
Roth, Julia. *Occidental Readings, Decolonial Practices: A Selection on Gender, Genre, and Coloniality in the Americas.* 2014. 284 pp.

| | | |
|---|---|---|
| WVT Wissenschaftlicher Verlag Trier | ISBN 978-3-86821-446-8 | € 26,50 |
| Bilingual Press / Editorial Bilingüe | ISBN 978-1-939743-07-7 | $ 32.50 |

Vol. 11
Thies, Sebastian, Gabriele Pisarz-Ramirez, and Luzelena Gutiérrez de Velasco, eds. *Of Fatherlands and Motherlands: Gender and Nation in the Americas / De Patrias y Matrias: Género y nación en las Américas.* 2015. 344 pp.

| | | |
|---|---|---|
| WVT Wissenschaftlicher Verlag Trier | ISBN 978-3-86821-528-1 | € 29,50 |
| Bilingual Press / Editorial Bilingüe | ISBN 978-1-939743-08-4 | $ 39.50 |

Vol. 12

Fuchs, Rebecca. *Caribbeanness as a Global Phenomenon: Junot Díaz, Edwidge Danticat, and Cristina García.* 2014. 298 pp.

| | | |
|---|---|---|
| WVT Wissenschaftlicher Verlag Trier | ISBN 978-3-86821-533-5 | € 26,50 |
| Bilingual Press / Editorial Bilingüe | ISBN 978-1-939743-09-1 | $ 32.50 |

Vol. 13

Andres, Julia. *¡Cuéntame algo! – Chicana Narrative Beyond the Borderlands.* 2015. 202 pp.

| | | |
|---|---|---|
| WVT Wissenschaftlicher Verlag Trier | ISBN 978-3-86821-569-4 | € 25,00 |
| Bilingual Press / Editorial Bilingüe | ISBN 978-1-939743-11-4 | $ 28.50 |

Vol. 14

Hertlein, Saskia. *Tales of Transformation: Emerging Adulthood, Migration, and Ethnicity in Contemporary American Literature.* 2014. 228 pp.

| | | |
|---|---|---|
| WVT Wissenschaftlicher Verlag Trier | ISBN 978-3-86821-570-0 | € 25,00 |
| Bilingual Press / Editorial Bilingüe | ISBN 978-1-939743-10-7 | $ 31.50 |

Vol. 15

Raab, Josef, and Saskia Hertlein, eds. *Spaces – Communities – Discourses: Charting Identity and Belonging in the Americas.* 2016. 382 pp.

| | | |
|---|---|---|
| WVT Wissenschaftlicher Verlag Trier | ISBN 978-3-86821-590-8 | € 29,50 |
| Bilingual Press / Editorial Bilingüe | ISBN 978-1-939743-13-8 | $ 39.50 |

Vol. 16

Mehring, Frank, ed. *The Mexico Diary: Winold Reiss between Vogue Mexico and Harlem Renaissance. An Illustrated Trilingual Edition with Commentary and Musical Interpretation* (includes color plates and audio CD). 2016. 244 pp.

| | | |
|---|---|---|
| WVT Wissenschaftlicher Verlag Trier | ISBN 978-3-86821-594-6 | € 29,50 |
| Bilingual Press / Editorial Bilingüe | ISBN 978-1-939743-14-5 | $ 39.50 |

Vol. 17

Raussert, Wilfried, Brian Rozema, Yolanda Campos, and Marius Littschwager, eds. *Key Tropes in Inter-American Studies: Perspectives from the* forum for inter-american research (fiar). 2015. 374 pp.

| | | |
|---|---|---|
| WVT Wissenschaftlicher Verlag Trier | ISBN 978-3-86821-627-1 | € 29,50 |
| Bilingual Press / Editorial Bilingüe | ISBN 978-1-939743-16-9 | $ 39.50 |

Vol. 19

Rehm, Lukas, Jochen Kemner, and Olaf Kaltmeier, eds. *Politics of Entanglement in the Americas: Connecting Transnational Flows and Local Perspectives.* 2017. 226 pp.

| | | |
|---|---|---|
| WVT Wissenschaftlicher Verlag Trier | ISBN 978-3-86821-675-2 | € 27,50 |
| Bilingual Press / Editorial Bilingüe | ISBN 978-1-939743-17-6 | $ 32.50 |

Vol. 20

Britt Arredondo, Christopher. *Imperial Idiocy: A Reflection on Forced Displacement in the Americas*. 2017. 194 pp.

| | | |
|---|---|---|
| WVT Wissenschaftlicher Verlag Trier | ISBN 978-3-86821-706-3 | € 26,50 |
| Bilingual Press / Editorial Bilingüe | ISBN 978-1-939743-20-6 | $ 30.00 |

Vol. 21

Schemien, Alexia. *Of Virgins, Curanderas, and Wrestler Saints: Un/Doing Religion in Contemporary Mexican American Literature*. 2018. 218 pp.

| | | |
|---|---|---|
| WVT Wissenschaftlicher Verlag Trier | ISBN 978-3-86821-724-7 | € 27,50 |
| Bilingual Press / Editorial Bilingüe | ISBN 978-1-939743-22-0 | $ 32.50 |

Vol. 22

Fulger, Maria Diana. *The Cuban Post-Socialist Exotic: Contemporary U.S. American Travel Narratives about Cuba*. 2020. 266 pp.

| | | |
|---|---|---|
| WVT Wissenschaftlicher Verlag Trier | ISBN 978-3-86821-769-8 | € 32,50 |
| Bilingual Press / Editorial Bilingüe | ISBN 978-1-939743-27-5 | $ 36.00 |

Vol. 23

Raussert, Wilfried, and Olaf Kaltmeier, eds. *InterAmerican Perspectives in the 21st Century. Festschrift in Honor of Josef Raab*. 2021. 320 pp.

| | | |
|---|---|---|
| WVT Wissenschaftlicher Verlag Trier | ISBN 978-3-86821-803-9 | € 32,50 |
| UNO University of New Orleans Press | ISBN 978-1-60801-211-4 | $ 36.00 |

Vol. 24

Kaltmeier, Olaf, Mirko Petersen, Wilfried Raussert, and Julia Roth, eds. *Cherishing the Past, Envisioning the Future. Entangled Practises of Heritage and Utopia in the Americas*. 2021. 176 pp.

| | | |
|---|---|---|
| WVT Wissenschaftlicher Verlag Trier | ISBN 978-3-86821-804-6 | € 23,50 |
| UNO University of New Orleans Press | ISBN 978-1-60801-206-0 | $ 27.50 |

Vol. 26

Raussert, Wilfried. *'What's Going On': How Music Shapes the Social*. 2021. 224 pp.

| | | |
|---|---|---|
| WVT Wissenschaftlicher Verlag Trier | ISBN 978-3-86821-811-4 | € 28,50 |
| UNO University of New Orleans Press | ISBN 978-1-60801-199-5 | $ 34.00 |

Vol. 27

Frank-Job, Barbara. *Immigration as a Process: Temporality Concepts in Blogs of Latin American Immigrants to Québec*. 2021. 138 pp.

| | | |
|---|---|---|
| WVT Wissenschaftlicher Verlag Trier | ISBN 978-3-86821-820-6 | € 20,00 |
| UNO University of New Orleans Press | ISBN 978-1-60801-215-2 | $ 24.00 |

Vol. 28

Roth, Julia. *Can Feminism Trump Populism? Right-Wing Trends and Intersectional Contestations in the Americas.* 2021. 168 pp.

WVT Wissenschaftlicher Verlag Trier      ISBN 978-3-86821-821-3      € 23,00
UNO University of New Orleans Press      ISBN 978-1-60801-205-3      $ 26.00

Vol. 30

Buitrago Valencia, Clara. *Missionaries: Migrants or Expatriates? Guatemalan Pentecostal Leaders in Los Angeles.* 2021. 236 pp.

WVT Wissenschaftlicher Verlag Trier      ISBN 978-3-86821-818-3      € 28,50
UNO University of New Orleans Press      ISBN 978-1-60801-210-7      $ 34.50

Vol. 31

Schwabe, Nicole. *De-Centering History Education: Creating Knowledge of Global Entanglements.* 2021. 92 pp.

WVT Wissenschaftlicher Verlag Trier      ISBN 978-3-86821-828-2      € 18,00
UNO University of New Orleans Press      ISBN 978-1-60801-214-5      $ 21.00

Vol. 32

Manke, Albert. *Coping with Discrimination and Exclusion. Experiences of Free Chinese Migrants in the Americas in a Transregional and Diachronic Perspective.* 2021. 162 pp.

WVT Wissenschaftlicher Verlag Trier      ISBN 978-3-86821-829-9      € 23,00
UNO University of New Orleans Press      ISBN 978-1-60801-207-7      $ 27.00

Vol. 33

Rohland, Eleonora. *Entangled Histories and the Environment? Socio-Environmental Transformations in the Caribbean, 1492-1800.* 2021. 92 pp.

WVT Wissenschaftlicher Verlag Trier      ISBN 978-3-86821-833-6      € 18,00
UNO University of New Orleans Press      ISBN 978-1-60801-208-4      $ 21.00

Vol. 34

Kaltmeier, Olaf. *National Parks from North to South. An Entangled History of Conservation and Colonization in Argentina.* 2021. 208 pp.

WVT Wissenschaftlicher Verlag Trier      ISBN 978-3-86821-834-3      € 27,50
UNO University of New Orleans Press      ISBN 978-1-60801-204-6      $ 32.50

Vol. 35

Raussert, Wilfried. *Off the Grid. Art Practices and Public Space.* 2021. 232 pp.

WVT Wissenschaftlicher Verlag Trier      ISBN 978-3-86821-835-0      € 29,50
UNO University of New Orleans Press      ISBN 978-1-60801-213-8      $ 34.50

Vol. 36
Ravasio, Paola. *This Train Is Not Bound for Glory. A Study of Literary Trainscapes.* 2021. 114 pp.

| | | |
|---|---|---|
| WVT Wissenschaftlicher Verlag Trier | ISBN 978-3-86821-836-7 | € 18,00 |
| UNO University of New Orleans Press | ISBN 978-1-60801-216-9 | $ 21.00 |

Vol. 37
Schäfer, Heinrich Wilhelm. *Protestant 'Sects' and the Spirit of (Anti-)Imperialism. Religious Entanglements in the Americas.* 2021. 242 pp.

| | | |
|---|---|---|
| WVT Wissenschaftlicher Verlag Trier | ISBN 978-3-86821-855-8 | € 29,50 |
| UNO University of New Orleans Press | ISBN 978-1-60801-209-1 | $ 34.50 |